an angry pen

*This lashing series of sixteen satiric verses fires
to life a society that flourished centuries
ago. Juvenal's impact is immediate: one reads of
living men and women. Whether he castigates the
Roman female, as in the famous Satire VI,
depicting her frail morality and violent excesses;
or despises the effeminate man, in Satire II,
Juvenal's genius catches the surge, the life,
the tempo of a civilization caught up in excess.
It was a civilization the satirist loved and
mourned, as he recorded for all time its lost
virtues, its self-corruption, its approaching doom.*

Literature of Ancient Rome
in MENTOR Books

THE SATYRICON *by Petronius*
  translated by William Arrowsmith

A classic recreation of Nero's pleasure-loving Rome by the cultured, cynic, Petronius. In a brilliant new translation. (#MP493—60¢)

THE METAMORPHOSES *by Ovid,*
  translated by Horace Gregory

Ovid's magnificent collection of legends and myths, translated into vital modern poetry. (#MT291—75¢)

THE AENEID *by Vergil,* translated by Patric Dickinson

The great Roman epic of adventure, war, and love, in a brilliant new verse translation by a noted English poet and classical scholar. (#MT348—75¢)

WAR COMMENTARIES OF CAESAR translated by Rex Warner

Julius Caesar's classic first-hand account of his military campaigns in an outstanding translation by the author of *The Young Caesar*. (#MT333—75¢)

TO OUR READERS: We welcome your request for our free catalog of SIGNET and MENTOR Books. If your dealer does not have the books you want, you may order them by mail, enclosing the list price plus 5¢ a copy to cover mailing. The New American Library of World Literature, Inc., P.O. Box 2310, Grand Central Station, New York, 10017.

the SATIRES OF JUVENAL

A NEW TRANSLATION
WITH AN
INTRODUCTION BY
HUBERT CREEKMORE

A MENTOR BOOK

PUBLISHED BY
THE NEW AMERICAN LIBRARY

MENTOR BOOKS are published *in the United States* by
The New American Library of World Literature, Inc.,
501 Madison Avenue, New York 22, New York,
in Canada by The New American Library of Canada Limited,
156 Front Street West, Toronto 1, Ontario,
in the United Kingdom by The New English Library Limited,
Barnard's Inn, Holborn, London, E.C. 1, England

contents

NOTE

I have used the Latin text of The Loeb Classical Library edition, revised, and the numbers in the margin refer in almost every instance to the line numbers in that text.

Here I wish to express my deepest appreciation to Dr. Ursula Schoenheim (Department of Classical Languages, Queens College, Flushing, New York) for her thorough and painstaking comments on the first version of this translation. Her sensitiveness to the nature of both Latin and English, in structure, precision, tone, relevancy, and spirit, and her sympathetic understanding of the problems of a translator have been invaluable to me. Without her aid, this would be a very different book, but needless to say, whatever defects may be in it can be blamed on me alone.

introduction

I

What Juvenal was, we know—the greatest satiric poet of the world. *Who* he was, however, is all but unknown. The few dependable biographical details are deduced from the text of his sixteen satires, and except for the dates of his birth and death— these dates, even, are conjectural—the data are of a minor sort. The life assigned to him is mostly assumption by modern scholars, based on research, and invention by the scholiasts who wrote more than two centuries after his death.

Only one of his contemporaries, Martial, even mentions his name, and he gives no indication that Juvenal was a poet. Martial left Rome in A.D. 98 to return to his native Spain, where he died about 102. Juvenal's first book (Satires I–V) was published around 110, so Martial never knew what the friend whom he called "eloquent" was to do in later life.

In his mid-forties, Juvenal apparently got fed up with the morals of his time and with contemporary poetry, as his first satire suggests, and burst forth in angry diatribes. Reading them today, we can sense that they were hardly calculated to win friends among the rulers, politicians, millionaires, writers, philosophers, socialites, sycophants, informers, and fakes of his day. This, to a large degree, may explain why no other Latin writer mentions him until the Christian propagandist Lactantius, early in the fourth century. From that time on, his name and fame grew. Just as Juvenal's examples (though not

his themes) for the most part are several decades
or a century removed from his era, so it took two
centuries for his poems to begin to find a wide audience. The same topics recur in cycles in our Western civilization, and most of his satires could be
adapted to twentieth-century society as easily as
Samuel Johnson adapted two of them (III and X)
to the society of eighteenth-century England and
many other poets in other lands to their times.

These facts, as revealed in his poems, are what
we know: His first satire was written about 100—
the date is based on the reference to the condemnation of Marius Priscus in January of that year. In
support of this date for Satire I, we have veiled attacks on the Emperor Domitian in Satire II*; and in
Satire IV the reference to his death in 96. In Satire
VI Juvenal refers to a comet and an earthquake as
omens connected with military affairs in Armenia
and Parthia, the date of which would be 115. The
opening of VII can, sensibly, refer only to Hadrian,
who became emperor in 117, though some scholars
disagree. The mention of the consul Fonteius as
holding office sixty years earlier, in XIII, would
place this poem in 127; and the mention of the
consul Juncus in XV also gives a date near 127.

Juvenal's poetry is also the source of information
concerning his own life. In Satire I he refers to the
barber who shaved him when he was "young"—that
is, according to Roman standards, before he was
forty-five. At the end of XI he says he is too old
to enjoy the games and that his "shriveled skin" just
wants to soak up the sun. Using such data as a
basis, together with collateral research, scholars
estimate his birth at 60 and his death at 131.

The last lines of III indicate that he was born in
Aquinum, and this is supported by the discovery in
the eighteenth century of a partially destroyed mar-

---

* See lines 29–33 concerning Julia. Domitian had a niece named
Julia. Domitian, for all his immorality, was also a censor of
morals.

ble tablet on the base of an altar to Ceres, lost since the 1840's. The inscription, as restored by scholars, says that D. Junius Juvenalis, captain of the First (?) Dalmatian battalion, mayor of Aquinum in the census year, and priest of the deified Vespasian, dedicated the offerings to Ceres at his own expense. Is this the poet as a young man? The initial (for Decimus) and the first two letters of Junius were obliterated. If this is Juvenal, it indicates that his family was prosperous, that he had had a short but successful army career, and that he was important in civic affairs. But when the voice of the satirist, aged forty-five, is raised in Rome, he is poor, a client haunting the vestibules of the rich to collect his dole. Obviously his plans for advancement after military service under the wing of the imperial court had collapsed, and he is bitter about the *nouveaux riches*, the foreigners, the corrupt aristocrats—everything.

Perhaps he married, but no one really knows. At any rate, he never mentions a wife.

From XV we know that he lived for a while in Egypt. Some have assumed that he commanded an army outpost there, others that he was banished to Egypt for writing a lampoon on Domitian's favorite actor and returned to Rome only after the emperor's death. The tradition of his exile began early and is much more probable than that of his command of an army garrison. It at least accounts for the loss of his inheritance, which would have been confiscated by Domitian.

Late in life he was apparently in comfortable circumstances, no longer railing so bitterly but in fact rather mellow and weary, though still with a bite in his voice. He had a farm near Tivoli (XI) and a town house with slave boys to help (XI and XII). Perhaps this was made possible by a pension from Hadrian, who may be the enlightened emperor of VII.

II

Hadrian was, excepting Vespasian and Trajan, the best of the emperors under whom Juvenal lived. In his early years, during Nero's reign, the poet could not have been impressed by imperial prerogatives and excesses, and in any case he was in Aquinum, not in Rome. But we may assume that even there people heard news of the court scandals. Nero was sixteen when he came to power, and though still under the influence of tutors, he promptly poisoned his rival, Britannicus. Later he murdered his mother and his wife, indulged in atrocities, perversions, and vicious tyranny, as well as in verse making and playacting on the stage. Faced with revolt and the defection of the praetorian guard in favor of Galba, he committed suicide.

In rapid succession four emperors were raised to the throne, all generals more than they were nobles, and all chosen by Roman armies rather than by the Senate or by a preceding ruler. The first, Galba, was killed within seven months by the praetorians who chose him. Next, Otho committed suicide after a reign of ninety-five days on learning that the armies in Germany had proclaimed Vitellius emperor. Vitellius held the throne only eight months before the armies in the east swore allegiance to Vespasian, whose soldiers, when they reached Rome, murdered Vitellius and brought the first of the Flavian line into power.

Such insecurity and disorder in the court were naturally reflected in the lives of the citizens; but they, unless involved in the intrigues for power, had become inured to imperial corruption. There were, of course, men of virtue, such as those whom Pliny the Younger dwells on in his letters, and men who were critical, such as Juvenal, Martial, and the historian Tacitus. To them the reign of Vespasian was a relief in the succession of sadistic tyrants. By nature rugged and rustic, Vespasian governed reasonably well considering that the general moral tone of society was still, as it had been for more than a century, degenerating. He at least died a natural death, and his popular son, Titus, succeeded him until his own death two years later. Titus' brother, Domitian, then became emperor, and tyranny, murder, cruel intrigues, and every sort of vice once again were the order of life in Rome.

Any man who dreamed that the country had left behind the depravities and savagery of Tiberius, Caligula, and Nero was sorely deluded. For fifteen years—those of Juvenal's young manhood—Domitian held the Roman Empire in the capricious grasp of a despot. Though he built and restored public buildings, expanded the empire, and was in his early reign seriously concerned with domestic affairs, he gave in to sycophants (see IV, in which Domitian is the emperor) and delators and devoted more of his attention, later on, to his "bed-wrestling exercises" and less to the diplomatic and constructive exercise of his office. After his assassination in 96, the Senate, seizing the opportunity, chose seventy-year-old Nerva, but he lasted only two years. He was followed by the moderate, progressive rule of Trajan, at whose death the calm, cultivated Hadrian, his ward, acceded to power.

Someone has remarked that it is incredible that Rome could have survived such emperors as were produced by the Julian and Flavian houses; it is even more incredible that Rome could have expanded in power and wealth for long afterward. That, however, occurred, and it was more than three centuries after Juvenal's death before the empire collapsed. More relevant to Juvenal, though, is a comment of Aurelius Victor, a fourth-century writer, that up to the time of Domitian's death emperors had been of Roman or Italian birth and that

henceforward they were foreigners.* It is for some
other branch of commentary to examine the reasons why the Romans, beginning with high moral
standards in every activity and with a republican
form of government, should have evolved into a
more and more corrupt society. The point to note
is that after Juvenal was forty, the two emperors he
lived under were "foreigners," a breed the poet
hated. Both Trajan and Hadrian were from Spain.
But so was Juvenal's friend Martial, whose hundreds
of brief poems make much the same bitter comment
on Roman life as those of Juvenal. These men were
not, however, the particular sort of foreigners
whom Juvenal detested and could epitomize as
Greek or Oriental or rich, usually with a background
of slavery.

Juvenal's resentment, we may assume, was against
those who had come in before and during Domitian's
reign, who represented license, perversion, new
manners, freed slaves risen to wealth, and in general the new rich. The truth is that Juvenal was cling-
ing to the standards of a bygone age in a time when
all was changing. He harks back to the days of the
republic, before Julius Caesar, when men were stern
in honor and morals and conduct, and he often
cites the early heroes of Rome. That he seems un-
realistic in this, since the change from the republic
to empire had been made almost a century before his birth, is only slightly surprising. Through all
of Roman poetry the harking back to the blessed
days of the golden age is a convention, and Juvenal
follows it. But it is one thing to describe, in line
with poetic tradition, the legendary diet of acorns,
the simple life, the modest home, the garden that
fed the family, and another thing to pit the early
heroes and "good kings" of Rome against the corrupt
rulers of his time. It is pointless to agree that Numa,

* Domitian's successor, Nerva, however, was not a foreigner, but
was born in Narnia in Umbria and was a praetor-elect under
Nero.

Gracchus, Fabius, Marcellus, Cato, Crassus, and others were nobler in every way than the lords of the society he knew. He was not alone in perceiving and registering violently in his writing the change in society that he did not understand: the incursions of new people—upstarts, but determined, energetic, unscrupulous, and, if they succeeded, rich. In one way or another, historians such as Tacitus and Suetonius and writers such as Martial and Petronius recorded the shift in Roman society, but none with anger and disgust to equal Juvenal's.

It seems a more serious criticism of Juvenal, the "conservative," the admirer of the "good old days," that he did not pinpoint the causes of the changes than that he exaggerated the results of the changes. Exaggeration is after all one of the techniques of satire. At the same time, we must recognize that the satirist is most concerned with what is, and not so much with why it is. If Juvenal seems to exaggerate the picture of his times, it might be well to consider the picture of our own times, which are so similar. Certainly there are people of virtue today, as there were then; but the general temper, the morals, the ethics ("the only crime is to get caught"), are little different. We see today that virtuous people condone and accept rather than reject and protest the stupidity, the ignorance, the extravagance, the profligacy, the chicanery, the double-dealing, and the crimes of all who are "big names" or powerful corporations. Today, as in ancient Rome, worship of wealth is, obviously, the common denominator between the man of virtue and the man of vice.

III

What Juvenal described but did not interpret in the life of Rome was an intertwined series of revolutions. The ranks of the senators, the nobility, the bulwark of the republic, had been shrinking for years; had capitulated to power factions; had decayed through their own debaucheries, perversions, and excesses; had been reduced to poverty by the emperors; or had extinguished their own lives and lineage by "opening their veins" in the face of imperial threat or command. Few nobles could expect to live to old age. It has been estimated that even in the reign of Claudius, three hundred knights and thirty-five senators were executed. Suetonius wrote that in Tiberius' reign, after the murder of Sejanus, there was at least one execution a day. How many more, then, might have vanished during the reigns of Caligula, Nero, and Domitian? Claudius had to include Venetian and Lombardian Gauls in the Senate because the aristocrats were so depleted, and Vespasian scoured Italy and the provinces for likely candidates to fill their ranks. To the decimation of the noble families by the emperors (who profited in this by proscription of their wealth), add those nobles who were homosexual and had no progeny, or none of substance, and those condemned to exile in distant provinces or islands; at length you have hardly anyone of a great family, or even of position, who also had some wealth. Except. . . . ?

Except the "new man"—the tradesman who had worked industriously and made a fortune while the aristocratic classes were scorning work and depending on the meager favors of rich patrons. This new class was made up of all those Juvenal loathed— the freedman, the Greek, the Oriental and African immigrant, slave or otherwise. Their becoming free of bondage, sometimes well-to-do in the process, was often related to the depravity of the noble class. And the emancipation of women, who heretofore had seldom ventured outside the house, was again a minor factor in the general depravity and laxity, as well as, in part, in the acceptance of homosexuals.

Juvenal's castigation of the "new woman" is contained in his longest, and to some his finest, poem,

Satire VI, which categorizes them within the framework of the question "Why get married?" This new woman was not actually so new, and had been emerging for many years. She was not the industrious, secluded, virtuous woman of early Rome; she moved about town as she wished, joined men at their dinners, schemed and murdered for wealth and power, and in general lived a life of her own. And like the men, if they were gentlemen, she was supremely idle—even idler than they were—so we can understand if not condone the ways she found to kill time.

Gentlemen in those days were not to be involved in trade; senators were not even allowed to be so involved, and this was the accepted view of Juvenal, who, though scarcely a gentleman, aspired to that status. They might be authors of prose or poetry, or teachers, or lawyers, but they could not descend to the disgrace of "work." That was left to slaves, freedmen, and immigrants, with what results we know only too well. Gentlemen, then, were busy, but not at "business." The emperor, the senators, and other officials, along with their assistants, had many demands and duties to meet. But for the rest, none of the gentle occupations brought in much money, so the learned or talented man, if he had no wealth, was reduced to becoming a "client" of a rich patron, who as often as not had made his fortune by degrading work. Though Juvenal deplored the client-patron relationship, the irony implicit in it seems almost to have escaped him. The client, at any rate, had a busy day—up at dawn for the rich man's levee and his dole, and then attendance on him throughout the day at lawcourts or recitations or discussions in the forum; and the client was also at all times busy minding his manners.

Yet, with all his scorn for work and for tradesmen and slaves, Juvenal overflows with sentiment for his own slaves, nobler in his eyes than the contemporary nobles; he praises the commoners and slaves of the republic who showed their patriotism in heroic deeds; and the whole of XII is woven around his friend Catullus, a tradesman, an importer, though the point of the poem is turned against flatterers and legacy hunters.

Legacy hunting, however, was virtually a profession, as were informing, falsely accusing, and bearing false witness. In fact, one could become a millionaire overnight if successful at delation. But even this vicious practice had been tolerated already for many decades.

We may agree, then, that none of Juvenal's material was new or characteristic of only his era. In Nero's day Petronius, in his prose *Satyricon,* had described the perversion, the low life, and the new-rich "climber" and perhaps in the lost books much else that would have paralleled Juvenal's subject matter. Before Petronius, the satirist Persius had treated some similar topics, but in a manner that smells of the library rather than the streets. The biographies of Suetonius, who was Hadrian's secretary, reveal the sordid sides of the emperors in a somewhat schematic way, but his guiding force was gossip. Among the writers of the century from Augustus through Hadrian, only Tacitus brings to his work an indignation comparable to that which imbues the writing of Juvenal. Martial, in his epigrams, exposes the vices and follies of the day, but his purpose was to shock, to sting, to entertain. The other authors who have survived as poets—and they are few—concentrated on safe themes such as historical or mythical heroes and events. Lucan versified *The Civil War (Pharsalia),* Statius wrote sweet thoughts in his *Silvae,* and Seneca wrote closet dramas in verse about Hercules, Medea, and other legendary figures. There is, however, one tragedy on a contemporary theme that was long attributed to Seneca —*Octavia,* which dealt with the daughter of Claudius and the wife of Nero, who put Octavia to death. In the face of such a widespread retreat from reality, it is no wonder that Juvenal burst out as he did in the opening of his first satire. When he began, not even Martial was around to stick a mere pin into the arrogant pretenders and villains. And the basic difference exists in their panoramas of Roman life: Martial made his out of hundreds of sketches, deft, brief, caustic, witty, and mocking; Juvenal, injured in body, heart, and soul by the society he lived in, painted a broad canvas full of indignation, denunciation, and passionate contempt, all of it shaped around moral judgments. His friend Martial may have provided the impetus; but Juvenal expanded his miniatures into full-scale pictures, organized on important if commonplace themes and sustained by detailed examples, and delivered a condemnation that is only implicit in Martial's work.

IV

The satires are written in dactylic hexameter, and Juvenal very likely read the first of them in much the same way that he describes in Satire VII. Later he published Book I, composed of I–V, in or after 110. Publication in those days meant a public recital or circulation of the manuscript to a number of friends. After that the manuscript was reproduced in copies for or by such friends as might wish to own the work. Copying was expensive if done professionally, however, and long before this time a class of "booksellers" had come into being, whose slaves were trained to copy manuscripts; they not only produced copies on commission but also pirated works and sold copies, with no royalty to the author, for fancy prices. Because the impoverished author could not afford such costs, the mere recitation of a work served usually as publication until there was a demand for copies. Juvenal's first book (a book meant what to us might be less than forty pages) opens with a sort of introduction—

"Why should I write satire?"—that gives a synthesis of the topics he covers in succeeding books. At the end of this first satire, he states that since he cannot name the names of contemporaries without fear of reprisal, he will use the names of the dead. Today this is of slight importance. After all, the cases were the same in his time and for a century before; and for us they are, in the shrinkage of past ages, to all effects as if coeval. After this prospectus, the other four satires treat the sexual and philosophical perversion of men, the hazards of life in the palace or slum that was Rome, the ridiculous concerns of Domitian as emperor, and the humiliation of native Romans by the new rich.

Book II is the long attack on women, made up only of Satire VI. Book III (Satires VII–IX) is concerned with the low condition of the man of learning and talent, with the folly of pride in lineage without personal virtues, and with a portrait of the most ignoble of any class, a whining male whore.

We begin Book IV (Satires X–XII) with a poem that ranks along with III and VI as one of Juvenal's best, and possibly because of its generally Christian temperament, a favorite in later times. Its unrelieved pessimism is balanced by the two following satires, one describing a dinner at home with a friend and the other a sacrifice made for the survival of a friend from shipwreck.

Wealth is a dominant theme in Book V (Satires XIII–XVI), published probably in 130, with the first two poems considering the default of a friend who held money in trust, and the ways by which parents train their children in avarice. Then follows a true story of cannibalism in Egypt, and finally there is the fragment dealing with the privileges of the army as against civilians.

We judge the satires today as separate poems rather than as components of a slim book, and their excellence of form varies, as do their vigor and passion, their vitality in the scenes of Roman life, and many other qualities. As has been noted, the favorites are VI, on marriage and women; III, on life in Rome; and X, on the vanity of human wishes. But all of them contain valuable, vivid insights into the hazards and corruption of social conditions in Juvenal's time that we would be the poorer without.

If Hadrian, as is assumed, gave Juvenal a post in his newly established Athenaeum, it is quite possible that the poet deposited a copy of his works in its library; and from that manuscript, long ago vanished, all the texts we now have were derived. It seems certain that only one copy of Juvenal's work survived long enough to be reproduced, for every one of the later manuscripts (there are some five hundred after the fourth century) ends at the same line of the unfinished sentence in Satire XVI. With a bit more neglect, Juvenal might easily have been completely lost to us. There are differences in the manuscripts, of course, and it is impossible to determine the number of deletions, rearrangements, and changes made. As recently as 1899 an unknown passage of thirty-four lines of VI was found in the Bodleian Library (known as the O fragment and so marked in recent texts).

Let us be thankful that we have Juvenal's work, for it is probably the most lively, brilliant firsthand report existent of life in this crucial, degenerate period of the Roman Empire. His character shows through the poems—bitter against shabby but rich pretenders, stanch for tradition and noble virtues, tender toward simple people and simple life, and hating all that was changing Rome from a mighty empire into a puny, proud nation of luxury. He was the last of the great pagan authors in Latin. The best Latin writers after him were Christian, and it was these Christians, ironically, who found so much in common, ethically and morally, between his poems and Christianity that they preserved and praised his work.

V

It has been noted already that the first mention of Juvenal after his death was by Lactantius in the fourth century. That Roman writers ignored him may be accounted for in the facts that life was comparably happy and that the later emperors espoused one or another of the characteristics that Juvenal attacked—they were pro-Greek or deranged or stupid or perverted. But Lactantius quoted him (much earlier, Tertullian, by obvious echoes, showed that he must have read him), and his fame gradually was spread by the Christian writers Ausonius, Paulinus of Nola, Prudentius, St. Jerome, and St. Augustine. After that, when copies of his satires were more easily available, Juvenal became better and better known and admired. Scholars worked at editing and collating texts and at adding marginalia and interpretations, from which developed the legends of his life.

Many writers of the medieval period were familiar with his work, and since they were in a sense bilingual, speaking Latin and a vernacular, bits of Juvenal appeared in Old French, Italian, and German. The times were ripe at last for his work to be appreciated, for its moral tone and denunciation fitted well into the prevailing Christian society. At length Dante, though not really familiar with all the satires, quoted from them and in his *Divine Comedy* consigned Juvenal fairly comfortably—for a pagan —to limbo. Dante's successors, Petrarch, Boccaccio, and Chaucer, knew, admired, quoted, and sometimes imitated Juvenal.

During the Renaissance, printing became possible; thus Juvenal reached a larger audience of talented readers, and his work was more widely imitated. Translation was inevitable after the many quotations and patent echoes in English authors and those of foreign tongues, and in the seventeenth century the first English translation appeared, done by Sir Robert Stapylton. Later John Dryden produced his versions, and in the nineteenth century there were still more. In other languages, the pattern was much the same, so that his voice became known over all the Western world.

Gilbert Highet, in his book on Juvenal, has said that "what he needs most is one or two good modern verse translations or adaptations—made without pedantry, eliminating or modernizing obsolete allusions, and putting the violence which characterizes so much contemporary literature into Juvenal's own more economical and more effective form." * This is a large, a fairly impossible order. He himself and others have noted that one cannot modernize the characters without danger of libel suits. One can only try, and see what comes out. Two of the best tries that I know are that of William Gifford in 1802 (*Satires*. Rev. ed. New York: E. P. Dutton and Company, Inc., 1954) and, more contemporary in every way, that of Rolfe Humphries (*Satires*. Bloomington: Indiana University Press, 1958).

VI

Two minor points remain to be mentioned. First, the impression that Juvenal has made on modern man, even when he is unaware of its source, is seen in the current widespread use of certain of his phrases and expressions. The chief of these, "A sound mind in a sound body," might well be attributed by some to the Bible or to Shakespeare. "Bread and circuses" (or "bread and the games") is, again, a common phrase. Two others we use in their Latin original—*rara avis* (rare bird) and

* Gilbert Highet, *Juvenal the Satirist*. (New York and London: Oxford University Press, 1954), p. 232.

cacoëthes scribendi ("the itch to write"). Often quoted are these: "Honesty's praised, then left to freeze"; "True nobility lies in virtue alone"; "No one sinks all at once to the lowest depths of sin"; "We live in a state of pretentious poverty"; "The censor punishes doves but readily pardons the crows"; and "Who's to guard the guards?" "We suffer the ills of a long peace" was a favorite of politicians; and the passage on how one mangy pig, one rotten grape ("apple" is more pertinent to our own use of the image), can infect all the others was much cited by ecclesiastics. The image of simple contentment in "lord of a single lizard" has appealed to many. A small anthology might be made of less familiar aphorisms, but here are a few: "No bad man is happy"; "It's foolish to rest on another man's fame"; "A man who has nothing can sing in the face of a thief"; "The more a thing costs, the more it's enjoyed"; "The smell of profit is clean and sweet, whatever the source."

Then, there is the matter of the authenticity of the two final satires, which has often been questioned. From the early days of interest in Juvenal's work, the last, fragmentary satire has been suspect. Some scholars would not accept that a man who had been in military service could satirize that service. Such pat reasoning seems absurd and evasive of the facts of human nature. What can a man satirize better than what he has experienced? And what man has not changed some of his attitudes over a span of fifty years? Satire XV was also once suspect because of what were assumed to be geographical errors about Egypt; but the whole story of the two towns has been verified by data from contemporary sources, and the location of the towns was established by the archeologist Flinders Petrie in 1895. Juvenal modified his attitude toward the emperors, the ruling class, and the rich from his first satires to his last. He changed from violent denunciation of homosexuals in II to tolerance, probably acceptance, as suggested in one passage of VI and in IX. How much more reasonable, then, to assume that forty-odd years after his youthful experience in the army, he had better sources to draw on. After all, as a boy he had known the sort of emperors the army chose; and his own youthful hopes, based on army service, had failed long before. Most of all, the satire is not complete, and it is likely that if Juvenal was in fact an officer of a Dalmatian battalion and that if the sixteenth satire were complete, we would find in it references to his personal experiences in that army corps.

But as he himself said: enough of digressions, and to the story—Juvenal's story of Rome in the late first and the early second century. These are the times of the emperors Trajan and Hadrian, though the poems reflect the earlier times of Nero and Domitian as well. His contemporaries for one reason or another apparently hoped to blot out all knowledge of his satires for the future, but most of his writing has come down to us for our delight and instruction. And though you, today, like Juvenal's contemporaries, may not like what you see in his gloomy mirror and may not find yourself in his picture, you will probably, as you should, see many people you know.

I

why write satire?

Must I be forever only a listener—
    never talk back,
Though bored so often by the *Theseid*
    of Cordus, the hack?
Is this man or that, without my revenge,
    to pour out a stream
Of love wails, farces, a saga of
    Telephus, ream on ream
To waste a whole day, or a hackneyed
    Orestes, now distending
All over the margins and onto the back,
    without ever ending?
No man knows his own house so well
    as I know the grove of Mars
And Vulcan's cave, close to where the
    cliffs of Aeolus are.
What the winds are doing, what souls
    Aeacus in hell torments,
From where someone is stealing that
    Golden Fleece, how immense
Are the ash trees Monychus hurls
    in battle—these epics bombard
Our eardrums, Fronto's sycamores
    shake, his statues are jarred,
And the constant reciting cracks
    marble pillars and pilasters.
You get the same kind of tripe
    from poets or poetasters.

I too had to learn that stuff in
    school, on pain of the rod;
I too in my speech gave hindsight
    advice to Sulla to nod
His dotage away in peace and private
    life. But today
It's surely stupid indulgence, when
    so many bardlets bray
All around, to spare the paper they're
    sure to desecrate.
Then why do I wish to foot it over
    the course where great
Lucilius drove his team? If you have
    the time and will try
To listen patiently, I'll tell you
    the reasons why.

[22] When limp-limbed eunuchs take wives;
    when husky Maevia slits
Wild boars in the games and clamps
    a spear between naked tits;
When a barber who scraped my beard in
    youth has a bigger pile
Of wealth than all the nobility;
    when that scum of the Nile,
Crispinus, ex-slave from Canopus,
    around his shoulder flings
A cloak of Tyrian cloth and wafts a
    hot-weather gold ring
In the air on his sweating finger,
    unable to bear thereupon
The extra weight of a heavier jewel—
    when this goes on,
It's hard to keep from writing satire.
    What paragon
Exists who has such restraint, such
    steely callousness
To the vices rampant in our city
    that he can suppress

Comment when lawyer Matho on a
    brand-new litter goes by,
Bulging all over the sides; and next
    a government spy
Who informed against his noble
    friend and soon will shred
From the blackmailed bluebloods,
    already eaten out and bled,
The little that's left—a man whom
    even Massa dreads,
Whom Carus must bribe, to whom a
    terrified actor must lend
His wife as peacemaker; and when you're
    cut out of wills by men
Who by their rigid night work inherit
    estates and wealth
From itchy old frumps who are rich
    in funds but poor in health—
The best way to get to the top—and
    now rise to social heaven?
Take two—Proculeius gets only one
    part, but Gillo eleven,
In strict proportion to the size of
    their instruments.
Let each take the price of his blood
    and turn pale in consequence
As a man who steps barefoot on a snake
    or waits in suspense
To give an oration at the harrowing
    Lyons contest.

Why tell how great a rage burns dry   [45]
    the heart in my breast
When this embezzler from his ward (he
    rents him, too,
For sodomy) jostles us with droves of
    slaves pushing through;
When Marius, sentenced by futile
    verdicts (what matters the shame

So long as he keeps the cash?), can
    revel and make fair game
Of the angry gods and, exiled, begin
    his cocktails at noon?
Triumphant province, well may you bewail
    this legal lampoon!

[51]   Am I to consider these topics not
    worthy a Horace's pen?
Shouldn't I hunt them down? Why keep
    on driveling again
Of Hercules, or Diomedes, or the
    bellows that rose
From the Minotaur, or Daedalus flying
    while Icarus goes
Plopping into the sea, when today the
    soft husband takes,
If the law won't let his wife inherit,
    the fee from rakes
And paramours, for he's adept at
    seeing no more
Than happens on the ceiling, and
    guarantees to snore
In his cups with a vigilant nose; or
    when some youngster thinks
He's entitled to have an army command,
    though his high jinks
Have squandered the family fortune,
    splurged on horses, and now,
A travesty of Achilles' great charioteer,
    he's allowed
To break all records—even his axles—
    in making a tour
Of the country roads to impress his
    trenchcoated paramour?

[63]   Aren't you incited to fill huge
    notebooks when you stand

28

At any street corner and see a litter
    by eight men manned,
Yet simple and open for all to inspect,
    and in it barefaced,
Lolling like some Maecenas, a forger
    of wills embraced
By café society now because he's
    rich from a quick
Shifting of legal papers and giving a
    seal ring a lick?

And then you see an imperious wife   [69]
    who serves good wines
To a thirsty husband, but in them a
    lizard's venom combines,
And surpassing Lucusta, teaches stupid
    housewives the way
To produce black corpses that were
    their husbands yesterday,
Yet face down all the rumors. So if
    you'd be a big shot,
Dare do what will land you on Alcatraz
    as likely as not,
Or at least in prison. Honesty's
    praised, then left to freeze.
Crime doesn't pay, except with huge
    mansions, gardens with trees,
Fine tables, and old silver cups
    with goats embossed on each piece.
Who can sleep when he knows of greedy
    daughters-in-law seduced,
Of brides already corrupted, of teen-age
    adulterers used
By rich matrons? If natural talent
    is lacking, anger will write
The lines as best it can, just as
    I—or Cluvienus—might.

[81] From the time when Deucalion rowed a
    skiff up the mountain slopes
(On the crest of the Flood, of course)
    to ask man's fate and hopes,
And the stones grew soft and warm
    with life when cast behind,
And Pyrrha showed naked girls to men,
    whatever mankind
Indulges in—his prayers, fears,
    diversions, rage,
Delights, and business—that is the
    medley of my page.
When has there ever been a heavier
    harvest of vice?
When has the gut of greed swelled fuller,
    when have dice
Had such attraction? Gamblers don't
    go with merely a purse
To bet at the table, they bring whole
    coffers to disburse.
What battles you see, with stewards—
    sergeants, I ought to say—
Passing the ammunition! Is this
    but a simple display
Of madness, to squander thousands and
    yet spend not a penny
On clothes for a frozen slave? Which
    of our sires built so many
Fine villas, or on seven courses dined
    alone? Nowadays,
Upon the threshold a small dole basket
    is set in place,
Over which a toga-wearing throng
    must fight. All the same,
The steward first inspects your face,
    afraid your claim
Isn't valid and that you're using
    someone else's name.
If you're known, you get your dole.
    He tells the butler to call

What's left of the Trojan peerage—
    even they crowd into the hall
Along with us. "Pay the praetor first!"
    "The tribune's here too!"
A freedman pushes ahead and says,
    "I'm first in the queue!
Why should I falter or fear to
    defend my place? I know
I was born beside the Euphrates,
    as holes in my ears would show
If I tried to deny I'd been a slave.
    But now I've got
Five shops that earn me four hundred
    thousand. And tell me what
A senator's rank confers that should
    be desired, when I've lots
More wealth than other rich freedmen,
    especially, by damn,
If senators hire out as shepherds
    and baby-sit for a lamb?"
So let tribunes wait, let money prevail,
    let him who came
But lately to town with the chalky
    feet of a slave lay claim
To priority over the sacred offices.
    For by all odds,
Majestic mighty Wealth is the holiest
    of our gods.
But as yet, Pernicious Money, you
    inhabit no shrine
Of your own, we've made no altar for
    you as for the benign
Old deities Peace and Honor, Virtue
    and Victory,
Or the one where storks croak answers
    to prayers—Harmony.

While the Big Boys at the end of
    the year tot up what their dole

[117]

31

Brings in, how much it swells their
    income, what will their old
Dependents do, who out of it have to
    get cloaks and shoes
And firewood and bread? A swarm of
    litters comes up and sues
For dimes. A husband drags a pregnant
    or sick wife there
To make the rounds. Another, with
    tricks of the trade to spare,
Brings an empty curtained litter as
    proxy to claim double shares.
"It's my wife," he says; "pay us quickly.
    What's the delay, young chap?
Stick your head out, Galla. Oh, well,
    never mind; she's taking a nap."

[127] Each day is distinguished by a lovely
    program of doings:
The dole is paid, then off to the
    forum for pleadings and suings
At Apollo's court to support their
    patron, then talk for a while
Beside the statues of heroes, among
    which a wealthy and vile
Egyptian has set up his own; around
    the broad base of this,
With no fear of arrest, you may do
    even more than merely piss.
Then the weary, aging retainers go
    from their patron's door,
And give up hope, though man's most
    enduring hope is for
A dinner. Now they must buy sorry
    cabbage and wood for heat.
Meanwhile, with no guests to lie on
    vacant couches and eat,
Their lord is gobbling the choicest
    game and fruits and fishes.

And off those tables of handsome,
    enormous antique dishes,
They eat up a whole inheritance in a
    single meal.
This will wipe out the parasites, for
    who can bear to deal
With such selfish luxury? What a
    gaping gullet to stuff
A whole boar inside—a beast made for
    banquets! You'll pay soon enough
The full price, my bloated friend,
    when you strip yourself and take
To the baths your undigested peacock,
    and start to ache.
From this, sudden death—an old man
    dead without making a will.
As the news flies round the salons,
    no eyes with tears are filled,
And angry friends, non-heirs, applaud
    as the hearse goes by.

The future will find no worse morals   [147]
    to add, no new follies to try;
Our descendants will desire and do
    the same things we've done.
All vice is now at its height; sail
    into it, Satirist, run
With canvas unfurled. Perhaps here
    you'll say, "But where will you find
The talent to match the subject?
    Where find the open mind
Our distant ancestors had, to write
    whatever their hot,
Angry passions wished? 'Whose name
    do I dare not utter? What
Does it matter whether Mucius forgives
    my words or not?' "
But write "Tigellinus" today and you'll
    blaze among pine sticks

Where all those others, standing
   upright, throats tightly fixed
To a stake, burn and smoke; and your
   corpse plows up a wide band
When it's dragged across the middle
   of the arena's sand.

[158] Then a man who poisoned three uncles
   may ride and look down on me
With contempt from his downy litter?
   "Of course. And when you see
Him passing, press your fingers against
   your lips; if a man
Says merely, 'That's the one,' he'll
   be an informer. You can
With safety match Aeneas and Turnus
   in war; no one's hurt
If you tell how Achilles died or how
   many a search was stirred
For Hylas, who fell in a well with
   his jug. But when in rage,
As though with drawn sword, Lucilius
   roars, the hearer, whose wage
Of sin lies cold in his conscience,
   burns, he sweats to hear
Of crimes he knows are true. This
   brings on anger and tears.
So consider all of these things before
   your trumpet sounds;
Once in arms, you can't repent and
   flee from the battleground."
Then I'll make a test of how much I
   may be allowed to say
Of lords whose ashes lie beside the
   Flaminian Way.

II

hypocrites and homosexuals

Let me out, let me flee to Siberia
    and the Arctic Sea
When such frauds as these, who imitate
    the austere Curii
But live like Bacchantes, dare to
    talk about morals. First
Of all, although you may find their homes
    about to burst
With plaster casts of Chrysippus,
    they're unlearned, untaught;
For he's the most perfect one among
    them all who has bought
A statue of Aristotle or Pittacus
    and who sees
That his shelves contain an original
    picture of Cleanthes.
Looks are deceiving. For what street
    isn't thick with a crowd
Of grim-faced queers? Do you rant
    at vileness when you're avowed
The most notorious ditch the Socratic
    buggers have plowed?
The hair on your body, the bristles
    along your arms, pretend
To show a tough he-man, yet the doctor
    can't help but grin
When you show a hairless ass to be
    cured of itching piles.

35

This type rarely talks; they love deep
    silence and choose hair styles
Cut even shorter than their eyebrows.
    Peribomius, though,
Is more open and honest. I say he
    was born like this. He shows
In his leers and his walk that he's
    a fairy. The frank display
Of such men arouses pity; their very
    madness today
Brings them a pardon. Worse by far
    are those who denounce
With Hercules' wrath such vice, and
    while they talk virtue, bounce
A stud on their wiggling behinds.
    "Am I to respect you when you,
Sextus," the pervert Varillus cries,
    "do just as I do?
How am I worse than you?" Let the
    well-shaped mock the knock-kneed,
The white the Negro; but who could
    bear the Gracchi to bleat
About sedition? Who won't confuse
    earth with heaven, sky
With sea if Verres show hate for a
    thief, or Milo decry
Cutthroats? Or if Clodius should
    condemn adultery,
Or if Catiline should blame Cethegus,
    or Sulla's three
Disciples denounce proscriptions?
    Such a man was he,
The adulterer, lately defiled by
    sexual intercourse
Straight out of the tragedies, who
    brought back into force
Those hated moral laws that must be
    feared by all men,
Even Venus and Mars—at a time when
    Julia, his niece, grown thin

From drugs to produce abortions, would
    ever so often pour
From her womb a gobbet that favored
    her uncle. Is it, therefore,
Not proper and right that the vilest
    of men despise the pack
Of fraudulent Scauri and if they get
    bitten bite right back?

Laronia couldn't put up with one of   [36]
    their sour-faced crowd
So often crying: "O Julian law, where
    are you now?
Are you asleep?" With a smile she
    answered, "O happy day
To bring such as you to correct our
    morals! Once more Rome may
Regain her decency. For Cato the
    Third, I'll swear,
Has come down from heaven! Nevertheless,
    just tell me where
You buy that *Eau de Sweet Boys* that
    reeks from the tuft of hair
At your neck? Don't be ashamed; tell
    me the name of the store.
If you're digging up laws and statutes,
    you ought to cite, before
All the rest, the Scantinian law
    against perversion. First
Take a look at what men do; examine
    it—they do worse
Wild things than women do, but they've
    got a majority,
Their ranks are steadfast; queers
    have a firm compact. There'll be
No example so monstrous as yours among
    our sex: never
Has Media licked at Cluvia, Flora at
    Catulla. However,

Hispo's pale from drilling—on top
    of and under young fellows.

[51] "Do we ever argue cases, do we know
    the law? Do our bellows
Shake rafters in your courtrooms?
    A few of us wrestle, a few
Eat diets of special meat to build up
    muscles. But you,
The whole lot, spin wool, tote your
    stint in baskets full of fleece,
And twist your well-charged spindles,
    to surpass Penelope's
And Arachne's gossamer weave, employing
    the very same skill
As a strumpet perched on a log. It's
    no secret why Hister's will
Left all to his freedman, why he
    gave, while alive, so much
To his wife. A girl who sleeps third
    in a big bed will get rich!
So marry, my girl, and don't talk;
    your secrets are worth a mint!
Why, after this, are we sentenced as
    lewd and incontinent?
The censor punishes doves but readily
    pardons crows."

[64] The make-believe Stoics trembled at
    hearing her disclose
The obvious truth, and fled. For
    wherein has Laronia lied?
But what won't other men do when,
    Creticus, you decide
To wear a toga of gauze, and with
    all astonished to see
Your clothes, you inveigh against women
    given to lechery.

Fabulla's an adulteress; you may
    sentence Carfinia, too,
If you will, but neither would wear
    a gown like that one on you.
"But it's July—I'm hot!" Then
    preside stark naked; there's less
Disgrace in just being crazy. Look
    at the way you dress,
Who might be heard expounding statutes,
    giving laws,
By men returning, with wounds still
    fresh, from victorious wars,
And hillbillies who laid down their
    plows! What wouldn't you cry
If you saw that gauze on a judge?
    It's proper for witnesses, I
Suppose, to wear chiffon? Keen,
    stanch champion of those
Who love freedom, Creticus, you're
    as transparent as your clothes!
This is a contagious disease, and it
    will spread and creep
To many more, as the mange of one pig,
    the scab of one sheep,
Infects the entire drove on the farm;
    as one grape seeps
Its livid blue into all of the bunch.
    Before long you'll
Dare something more disgraceful than
    wearing a robe of tulle;
No one sinks all at once to the lowest
    depths of sin.

You'll gradually be accepted by cliques   [84]
    at homes wherein
They deck themselves with tiaras and
    ribbons on their brows
And necklaces round their throats,
    and worship with dugs of sows

And huge wine bowls the Good Goddess;
    but by their perverted rule
Real women are chased off and may not
    pass the vestibule.
This goddess's shrine is *For Men Only.*
    "Stay out," they warn,
"You unholy females! We need no
    women to blow our horns."
Like this were the secret torchlit
    orgies the Baptae pursued,
Which bored Cotytto of Athens, goddess
    of all that's lewd.
One swish is doing his eyes, painting
    lashes and brows
With mascara and tinting the trembling
    lids. Another bows
His lips to a phallic goblet, winds
    his long hair in a snood
Of golden mesh; he's wearing a drag
    of rainbow-hued
Big checks or perhaps of chartreuse
    velvet; the masculine maid
Like his master swears by Juno.
    Another holds an inlaid
Mirror such as Otho the Homo raised
    in his hands—
"The spoil of Auruncan Actor"—in
    which he gave a glance
At his armor before commanding his
    soldiers to advance.
Something new has been added, which
    history shouldn't bypass—
A soldier's gear is substandard
    without a looking glass!
It really took a fine general to kill
    Galba and still
Keep his own skin from roughness,
    a man of supreme strong will
To affect the palace pretensions out
    on Bebriacum's field

And smear his face with beauty packs!
    With quiver and shield,
Semiramis never did that in her
    Assyrian land,
Nor depressed Cleopatra on her ship
    with Actium at hand.
There's no decent language here,
    no table manners, no wit,
Only lewdness of speech and high, lisping
    voices well fit
To Cybele's priests, and an old fanatical
    man with white hair
Who acts as priest in the rites—an
    example, noteworthy and rare,
Of enormous intake and a teacher all
    should hire! But why
Are they waiting? Isn't it now high
    time for them to try
The Phrygian fashion and to make the
    job complete—
Take a knife and lop off that
    superfluous piece of meat?

Gracchus has settled four hundred   [117]
    thousand on a lowborn
Trumpet player—or maybe he blows a
    straight, stiff horn.
The license, the contract, are signed.
    "Congratulations!" Then
A huge reception. The "bride" is
    lying snugly within
Her husband's arms. O nobles, are
    soothsayers what we need,
Or is it a censor? Would you dread
    it more or read
It as a more monstrous sign if a woman
    birthed a calf,
Or a cow a lamb? The man who, when
    he carried the staff

And swaying shields of Mars by the
    sacred thongs, used to sweat
In holy processions now is dressing
    himself in the net
Of a wedding gown, with ruffles,
    a train, and a bridal veil!

[126] O Romulus, where did such wickedness
    come from to assail
Your shepherds? How, O Mars, did
    this itch spread to your sons?
Just look—a rich man of high birth
    wed to a man, yet not once
Do you shake your helmet in wrath
    or strike earth with your spear
Or even protest to your father.
    Well, then, get out of here;
Give up the wide, rugged field that
    you yourself neglect!

[132] "There's a ceremony tomorrow at dawn—I
    must pay my respects—
In the Quirinal valley." "What's the
    occasion?" "Why ask? A man
I know is to marry a husband; just
    a few guests on hand."
If we live long enough, we'll see
    such mates in public united;
They'll want it recorded in the papers.
    Meanwhile, these blighted
Brides are stuck with a problem that
    brings them great dismay:
They can't have babies to chain the
    husbands who might go astray.
For Nature's done well in this, to
    allow their bodies no way
To fulfill this desire; and sterile
    they die, for there's no aid

In sex pills from Lyde, the fat old
    quack, or in getting flayed
On the hand with magic whips by running
    Lupercan priests.

Here's a worse portent: Gracchus, wearing   [143]
    a tunic, was pleased
To ape a low gladiator and, waving a
    trident, run
All around the arena—a man of nobler
    birth than the sons
Of ancient houses, or of Marcellus
    or the offspring
Of Catulus, Paulus, or Fabius, nobler
    than the whole ring
Of well-born spectators in the loges;
    and don't forget
The man who paid for the show where
    he cast that shameful net.

The notion that there are such things   [149]
    as spirits of the dead,
And kingdoms under the earth, and
    Stygian streams bespread
With black frogs, and all those thousands
    crossing in one boat,
No boys believe except those too
    young to pay a groat
For the baths. But suppose that it
    were true: What would Curius and both
The Scipios think; and what would
    Fabricius and the ghost
Of Camillus, the legion slain at the
    Cremera, or the host
Of youth that fell at Cannae, all
    those brave hearts, feel
When a shade like Gracchus came among
    them? They'd appeal

For rites of purification if sulfur
    were only around
And torches and branches of wet
    laurel could be found.

[159] To such degradation we've come! We've
    pushed a mighty force
To the newly captured Orkneys past
    green Ireland's shores,
To Britain, whose people like the
    shortness of their nights.
But those we've conquered would never
    do the things that delight
The men of our victorious city.
    And yet they say
That Zalaces, a boy from Armenia,
    more girlish in every way
Than our young men, gave himself to
    a lusting tribune. See
What evil contacts do: He came here
    a hostage, but we
In Rome *make men*. If boys remain
    in our city long,
They'll never lack a lover. They'll
    abandon as wrong
Their trousers, bridles, knives, and
    whips and then take home
To Artaxata the customs of our youth
    in Rome.

III

the perils of life in rome

Although I'm sad at my old friend's
     departure, yet I praise
His purpose to make his home in
     abandoned Cumae and raise
The count of citizens of the Sibyl
     by one. For there
Lies the threshold to Baiae, a welcome
     resort on a fair
And pleasant shore. I'd even choose
     a desert isle,
Myself, to midtown Rome. For what
     place have we seen so vile,
So lonely, that you would not consider
     that it's much worse
To dread the constant fires and
     tumbling houses, the curse
Of our terrible city's countless perils,
     and the verse
That poets pour out in the month of
     August in cataracts?

But while all his goods on a single   [10]
     cart are being packed,
He stops at the old gate where the
     aqueduct drips overhead.
And here, where Numa once trysted
     with his beloved in dead

45

Of night, the sacred spring, the
    grove, and the shrine today
Are rented to Jews, who own just a
    basket and some hay.
For when each tree must pay the people
    a fee, the grove
Itself, with the Muses pushed out,
    has become a beggarly drove.
We go down to Egeria's vale and the
    caves—a parody
Of nature. How much closer the nymph
    of the spring would be
If borders of green grass edged the
    water instead of blocks
Of polished marble that heap insult
    on the native rocks!

[21]   Umbricius here spoke out: "Since
        there's no room," he commenced,
"For honest professions in this city,
    no recompense
For work, since my assets are less
    today than yesterday
And tomorrow will rub from what little's
    left a bit more away,
I've decided to go where Daedalus shed
    his exhausted wings
While the gray in my hair is new,
    while erect though entering
Old age, while some of my life's long
    thread may still remain
For Lachesis to spin and I can stand
    on my feet with no cane
In hand. Good-bye, my homeland!
    Let Artorius live there,
And Catulus; led those who turn black
    to white but turn not a hair
At contracting for temples, rivers,
    harbors, unclogging sewers,

Trundling corpses to pyres, or selling
    slaves to viewers
Under their spear of authority stay.
    These men, who once
Were horn tooters playing around the
    yokel circuit, whose grunts
And puffed-out cheeks were known in
    every tank town, today
Produce their own shows, and to delighted
    applause they slay
Whomever the mob with a twist of the
    thumb selects as prey.
Then back they go to contracts for
    flushing privies—why not?
Why not worse things? After all,
    they're the sort who were begot
In gutters, the sort that Fortune loves
    to lift up and cloak
With highest success whenever she
    wants to laugh at a joke!

"What's there in Rome for me to do?   [41]
    I'm not trained to lie.
I can't praise a book if it's bad
    and beg for a copy. And I
Know nothing about the movements of
    stars. I can't and I won't,
To any man, make the promise his father
    will die; I don't
Inspect, and never did, the entrails
    of a toad.
Let others learn to bring to a bride
    the gifts bestowed,
The letters sent, by her paramour.
    No man will pursue
A robbery with my help, so I leave
    in the retinue
Of no magistrate, like a crippled,
    useless body with dead,

Slack hands. Who's favored today
    except an accomplice with dread
Secrets boiling and burning inside
    his soul that must
Not ever be revealed? Nobody who has
    in trust
Made you a party to an innocent
    secret believes
He owes you anything, nor will you
    ever receive
A favor from him: the man that Verres
    will love is the man
Who can accuse Verres whenever it
    suits his plan.
Don't let the gold in the sand that the
    shady Tagus sweeps
To the sea become so precious to you
    that you can't sleep,
And to your sorrow take gifts, which
    must be left sometime,
And forever live as a threat to your
    powerful patron in crime.

[58]   "I'll hasten to say what race is most
    welcome to our millionaires
Today, one that I especially shun.
    No bashful care
Shall stop me. O Romans, I can't stand
    a Rome so Greekified.
But what a small part of our dregs
    is Greek! Long ago the wide
Orontes of Syria poured into the Tiber
    and brought
With its lingo and morals its flutes
    and harps with taut,
Oblique strings and its native
    tambourines and its bitches,
Ordered to hustle at the circus cribs.
    If your itch is

48

To fondle exotic whores in gaudy
    turbans, go there!
Your country cousin, Romulus, chooses
    now to wear
A dinner coat from Savile Row, Athens;
    his chest he trims
With *médailles d'honneur,* his neck
    is reeking *Parfum du Gym.*
One comes from high Sicyon, one from
    Andros, Tralles, or Samos,
Others from Amydon or Alabanda; all
    head for the famous
Esquiline Hill or Osier Heights to
    worm their way
To the heart of the finest homes and
    end as master some day.
They're quick-witted, brash, to all
    shame lost, and ready with lots
Of talk, in greater floods than
    Isaeus poured. But say, what
Do you think that fellow over there
    might be? His career
Is being whatever you wish—schoolmaster,
    masseur, engineer,
Physician, magician, ropedancer,
    palmist, painter, fall guy.
When hungry, our Greekie knows everything.
    Just tell him to fly,
He'll do it. After all, that man who
    spread wings on the breeze
Wasn't Moorish, Turkish, or Russian,
    but born in the heart of Greece.

"Shouldn't I flee these purple-garbed   [81]
    fops? Is he to sign
His name before me and upon a better
    couch recline
At the table who was brought to Rome
    by the Orient wind,

Imported with sundried figs and prunes?
        Does it count, in the end,
For nothing at all that as a baby I
        drank in the air
Of the Aventine Hill and was nourished
        on Sabine olives there?

[86]   "In the school of base flattery, these
        creatures are Ph.D.'s:
They praise the talk of a fool, the
        charm of a face that would freeze;
And compare the turkey neck of a
        milksop to Hercules' girth
Of shoulders, lifting Antaeus to death
        high over the earth;
And admire a squawking voice no
        sweeter than that of a cock
When pecking the hen he chose to service
        from all the flock.
We can praise the same things they do,
        but only they are believed.
Could any actor play Thaïs better,
        could one have conceived
The role of a wife with finer art, or
        a sea nymph naked
As a worm? You'd never think a made-up
        man could fake it
So well—a woman above and beneath
        the belly—and show,
Instead of a bulge at the crotch, a
        feminine crease below.
Yet back at home, Antiochus won't be
        noticed—a factor
That all these players face: that
        nation's a troupe of actors!
Grin and a Greek laughs with you; he
        splits his sides. He'll sob
If he sees his patron tearful—but not
        in grief; it's his job.

If you ask for a tiny fire in winter,
    he'll scurry and get
His cloak to keep himself warm. Just say,
    'I'm hot,' he'll sweat.
So there's no match between us. He's
    always got the best odds,
Ready both day and night to reflect
    the mood of such clods,
To throw up his hands in wonder and
    give his friend bravos
If he but belches deeply or, without
    wetting his clothes,
He pisses straight or, turning his
    golden bowl bottoms up,
He gurgles in one great gulp the whole
    contents of the cup.

"In addition, he thinks no one too
    sacred to honor his penis—
The mother, the virgin daughter, her
    fiancé who at eighteen is
Unshaven still, nor the son whom sex
    has yet to touch.
If these aren't handy, he'll rape his
    friend's grandma. Inasmuch
As he wants to learn the family secrets,
    he's someone to fear.
And now that I'm talking of Greeks,
    consider their schools and hear
Of crime in a doctor's cap and gown:
    the old Stoic Egnatius,
Who by informing on him murdered
    Barea, his gracious
Disciple and friend, was whelped on
    the banks where Pegasus dropped
One feather beside the river. When
    Rome can so proudly adopt
This flotsam of Greeks, there's no
    place for a Roman in town,

[109]

51

Where some Protogenes, Diphilus, or
    Hermarchus lays down
The law and, true to his racial faults,
    never shares a friend,
But keeps him all to himself. For
    once he has sneaked a blend
Of his own and his country's poison
    into an indulgent ear,
I'm shown the door, and my long years
    of service all disappear
In thin air. Nowhere is a client more
    lightly tossed overboard.

[126] "And anyway, what does a poor man's
    service in Rome afford—
Not to flatter ourselves—though he
    trouble to put on his toga well
Before dawn and hurry along to forestall
    the praetor who tells
His guards to go full speed to prevent
    his opposite number
From being the first to greet the
    childless, long waked from slumber
Albina and Modia? Here sons of natives
    yield right-of-way
To a rich man's slave, for he squanders
    as much as a colonel's pay
To quiver once in a while on top of
    Calvina or
Perhaps Catiena. But you, if you have
    a yearning for
Some bedizened harlot whose face you
    like, you just don't dare,
Being short on funds, to ask her to
    leave her high sedan chair.
Bring a witness to court in Rome, as
    trusty and undepraved
As Scipio who harbored the goddess of
    Ida, Metellus who saved

The frightened Minerva from the fire
    in her shrine, or bring out
Even Numa himself, the first question
    they ask will be about
His wealth, the last about his character.
    'How many slaves
Does he keep?' 'How much farmland
    does he own?' 'How many engraved
Dessert plates does he eat from? How
    big are they?' A man's word
Is believed just to the extent of the
    wealth in his coffers stored.
Though he swear on all the altars
    from here to Samothrace,
A poor man isn't believed—he has
    nothing to lose in case
The gods dart lightning, and they
    forgive him with good grace.

"Anyway, a poor man's the butt of   [147]
    jokes if his cloak has a rip
Or is dirty, if his toga is slightly
    soiled, if a strip
Of leather is split in his shoes and
    gapes, if coarse thread shows
New stitches patching not one but
    many holes. Of the woes
Of unhappy poverty, none is more difficult
    to bear
Than that it heaps men with ridicule.
    Says an usher, 'How dare
You sit there? Get out of the rows
    reserved for knights to share,
All of you whose means aren't enough
    under law! And let sons of pimps,
Born in brothels, take seats; let an
    auctioneer's son, well primped,
Applaud with a gladiator's dapper sons
    and the Ivy League sons

Of a gym trainer.' This distinction
　　of rich and poor was begun
By that idiot Otho. What son-in-law
　　here was approved on merits
If his money was less than the girl's?
　　What poor man ever inherits
A fortune or gets appointed as clerk
　　to a magistrate?
Long ago the penniless Romans ought
　　to have staged a great
Mass walkout. It's no easy job for
　　a man to advance
When his talents are balked by his
　　impoverished circumstance,
But in Rome it's harder than elsewhere:
　　high rent for tenements,
Fat budgets to feed your slaves' lean
　　bellies, and equal expense
For your own potluck. You're ashamed
　　to eat off earthenware;
But you wouldn't feel so if suddenly
　　set to country fare
Far off, where you'd love to wear a
　　coarse cape of Venetian blue.

[171] "In most Italian regions—we both
　　must admit it's true—
No man wears a toga until he's dead.
　　And even on days
Of festival, when green turf makes
　　a good theater for plays,
And a comedy hit is revived, and a
　　rustic babe at the breast
Is scared by slits in the ashen masks,
　　you'll see them dressed
Alike in front rows or rear—white
　　tunics are noble enough
For high magistrates' great office.
　　But here, in splendid stuff,

54

Beyond our means, we dress; and we
    buy it on the cuff,
We buy too much, to impress. It's a
    common fault hereabout—
We all live in pretentious poverty.
    Why not speak out?
Everything in Rome has a price.
    How much does it cost you to bow
To Cossus once in a while, or to get
    one glance somehow
From shut-mouth Veiento? The former's
    busy having a shave,
The latter is dedicating a lock from
    his favorite slave
At the altar. The house is full of
    feast cakes—at a price.
Take your cake or not, you'll
    take a slow burn, because to bribe
A tycoon we're forced to pay bribes
    to his whole fat menial tribe.

"In cool Praeneste or the verdant hills   [190]
    of Volsinii, who
Has ever feared his house would
    collapse as we all do—
Or in simple Gabii or Tivoli's craggy
    heights? But here
We live in a city held up for the
    greater part by mere
Toothpicks, for thus the janitor props
    the tottering beams
And patches up the old walls at cracks
    and gaping seams,
And tells the tenants to rest in
    peace—well said, 'R.I.P.,'
With rafters ready to cave in on their
    heads! Not for me!
I must live where there are no fires
    and no alarms in the night.

Below, some Ucalegon already is shouting
    in fright
For water and moving his stuff. From
    your attic room, smoke pours,
But you don't know it; for if the fire
    starts on the lower floors,
The last one to burn will be the man
    with nothing to keep
Him from the rain but the roof tiles,
    beneath which, in a heap,
The soft rock-doves lay eggs. The one
    bed that Codrus owned
Was too small for a dwarf, his cupboard
    boasted six mugs, a lone
Pitcher, a Chiron reclining, made of
    the same soft stone,
With an old chest of Greek books, whose
    lovely poems were chewed
By illiterate mice. Poor Codrus had
    nothing—isn't it true?—
But still he lost the whole nothing.
    The straw on the camel's back
Is this: although he's stripped of all
    and begging a snack,
No one will give him a paltry
    handout, no one a bed,
Or even offer him shelter, a roof above
    his head.

[212] "But let the great house of Asturicus
    catch and burn,
The matrons mourn, the nobles wear
    black, the courts adjourn.
Oh, then we bewail the city's disasters
    and hate its fires!
The palace is still in flames and
    someone runs up and desires
To give him marble or building funds,
    another is pleased

To offer shining nude statues, another
    a masterpiece
Of Euphranor or Polyclitus or figures
    of bronze from nooks
In ancient Asian temples. And others
    will give him books,
Bookshelves, a bust of Minerva, or
    silver in coin or plate.
This is how Persicus, most refined
    and most fortunate
Of the childless, restores his loss
    with more and richer things.
No wonder that he's suspected of
    arson—look what it brings!

"If you can be torn from the games,   [223]
    you can buy a fine house and stay
In Sora, Frusino, or anywhere else for
    what you now pay
In Rome to rent a dark hole one year.
    You'll have a small lawn,
A garden, a shallow well from which
    water is easily drawn,
With no need of ropes, to wet your
    tender plants. Live in peace
With a hoe as companion there, grow
    a truck garden fit to feast
A Vegetarian convention. Remote
    though your farm may be,
It's something to be the lord of one
    green lizard—and free.

"Here most of the sick die off because   [232]
    they get no sleep
(But the sickness is brought on by
    the undigested heap
Of sour food in their burning stomachs),
    for what rented flat

Allows you to sleep? Only rich men
    in this city have that.
There lies the root of the illness—
    carts rumbling in narrow streets
And cursing drivers stalled in a
    traffic jam—it defeats
All hope of rest. Even Drusus and
    sea cows are kept awake.
When a rich man has a business appointment,
    the crowd will make
A path for him to be carried above
    their heads in a rich
Liburnian litter. He reads or scribbles,
    no matter which,
As he goes along, or into the downy
    pillows he sinks,
With the litter's curtains closed,
    and snatches forty winks.
But he gets there before us. Though
    we hurry, we merely crawl;
We're blocked by a surging mass ahead,
    a pushing wall
Of people behind. A man jabs me,
    elbowing through, one socks
A chair pole against me, one cracks
    my skull with a beam, one knocks
A wine cask against my ear. My legs
    are caked with splashing
Mud, from all sides the weight of
    enormous feet comes smashing
On mine, and a soldier stamps his
    hobnails through to my sole.

[249] "Look at that cloud of clients
    scrambling to grab the dole—
A hundred guests with portable kitchens!
    Even Steve Reeves
Couldn't lift the weight of the brazier
    the little slave boy heaves

To his head, with casseroles hot on
    top, and carries with steady
Balance while running to fan the flames.
    Tunics, already
Newly mended, are ripped again. A
    huge fir log sways
On the wagon hauling it along; and
    next the drays
Of pine trees, towering, tottering,
    threaten all in their road
With death. For suppose an axle breaks
    beneath that load
Of Ligurian marble and lets a whole
    quarried mountain slide
Down on the crowd; what's left of
    their bodies? Who can divide
The limbs, the bones, of one from the
    rest? The pedestrian's crushed
Cadaver vanishes utterly, like his
    soul. And just
As his household, meanwhile, all unawares,
    is washing bowls
And platters, clattering greasy strigils,
    puffing the coals,
Refilling oil cruets, and laying out
    towels, and while unwitting
Slave boys scurry about, their master
    already is sitting
Beside the Styx, a newcomer, scared
    of the foul ferryman.
The poor wretch has in his mouth no
    penny to pay him, and
Therefore no hope of a passage over
    that murky stream.

"Now look at the other and varied   [268]
    perils of night: What extreme
Height to the lofty roofs from which
    a piece of a pot

Falls down on my head, how often a
    broken vessel is shot
From the upper windows, with what a
    force it strikes and dints
The cobblestones! If you go out to
    dinner without long since
Having made a will, you'll be thought
    a fool, reckless of fate
And sudden disaster; for as many sure
    deaths are lying in wait
In the night as the open windows you
    pass beneath on the street.
So you hope and plaintively pray they
    may be content to treat
You to showers of no more than what's
    in their full slop jars.

[278] "The besotted bully, denied his chance
    in the shabby bars
Of killing somebody, suffers torments,
    itching to fight.
Like Achilles bemoaning his friend,
    he tosses about all night,
Now flat on his face, now on his
    back—there's no way at all
He can rest, for some men can't sleep
    till after a bloody brawl.
But however rash and hot with youth
    and flushed with wine,
He avoids the noble whose crimson
    cloak and long double line
Of guards with brass lamps and torches
    show they're too much to handle.
But for me, whom the moon escorts,
    or the feeble light of a candle
Whose wick I husband and trim—he has
    no respect for me.
Now hear how the pitiful fight begins—
    if a fight it be,

When he delivers the punches and I
    am beaten to pulp.
He blocks my way and tells me to stop.
    I stop, with a gulp—
What else can you do when a madman
    stronger than you attacks?
'Where you from?' he roars. 'Whose
    dago red and beans have packed
Your bloated belly? What cobbler fed
    you sheep jowls and chopped leeks?
No answer? Talk, or I'll kick your
    behind! All right now, speak!
Where's your beat for begging? Tell
    me from what synagogue you came?'
You can try to speak or escape in silence,
    it's all the same—
He'll beat you up anyhow, then in
    rage he'll sue for assault.
This is the poor man's freedom: having
    been soundly mauled
And cut to pieces by fists, he begs
    and prays, half dead,
To be allowed to go home with a few
    teeth still in his head.

"But these aren't your only terrors.   [302]
    For you can never restrain
The criminal element. Lock up your
    house, put bolt and chain
On your shop, but when all's quiet,
    someone will rob you or he'll
Be a cutthroat perhaps and do you
    in quickly with cold steel.
For as long as the Pontine swamps and
    the Gallinarian woods
Are guarded by armed police, their
    denizens, killers and hoods,
All rush here as into a game preserve.
    What furnace in town,

61

What anvil isn't forging their heavy
    chains? That's how
Most of our iron is used—in fetters!
    Well may you fear
That none will be left for plowshares,
    hoes, or spades in a year.
You'd call our forefathers' ancestors
    happy, and happy besides
Those times that long ago, under
    kings and tribunes, in pride
Saw Rome with only a single jail
    well satisfied.

[315]   "I could add to this many other
    reasons, but I must go.
My wagon and team have started, the
    sun is slanting low,
My muleteer keeps waving his whip
    for me to come. So good-bye;
Don't forget me. And if some day you
    need a vacation and fly
From Rome to your own Aquinum, summon
    me too from my nest
In Cumae to your Diana and Helvine
    Ceres. Dressed
In jerkin and boots, I'll come to
    the cold land of your sires,
An audience of one, if deserving the
    honor, for your satires."

IV

council of state —
what to do with a fish

Look here, once again Crispinus!
    I'll often have to call
Him onto my stage, this monster of
    evil without one small
Redeeming virtue, this low debauchee,
    diseased and dread,
Strong only in lust that scorns no
    one except the unwed.
What does it matter, then, how big
    are the colonnades
That tire his horses, how broad the
    woods where he drives in shade,
How many lots near the forum, how many
    mansions, he's bought?
No bad man is happy, least of all a
    seducer who's brought
To incest, with whom a filleted
    priestess lately has lain,
To be, for that, interred while blood
    still pulsed in her veins.

But to lighter matters. Although if
    another had done the same,   [11]
He'd fall in the censor's grasp; for
    what would be called a shame

63

In Tom, Dick, or Harry became in
    Crispinus simply a grace.
What can you do when any charge you
    can bring him to face
Is less dreadful and foul than the
    man himself? He bought a mullet
For three hundred dollars—something
    like fifty a pound, as they would put it
Who want to exaggerate and make up
    a real fish tale.
I'd praise the cunning of his schemes
    if he prevailed
By any such costly gift upon a
    childless old man
To name him first in his will, or
    for better reasons, planned
To send it to some fine doxy who
    shuns the public glance
Behind shades of a litter with
    picture windows. Not a chance:
He bought it all for himself. We see
    a lot of things done
Today that the frugal glutton Apicius
    would have shunned.
Crispinus, did you, who formerly
    wore a G-string supplied
By your native papyrus, pay that price
    for a fish? You might
Have purchased the fisherman himself
    perhaps for less
Than the fish; and for the same amount
    you could possess
A farm in the provinces or a bigger
    estate like those
Down in Apulia. What sort of feasts
    must we suppose
The emperor himself gobbled up
    when by a parasite duke
In purple of palace pomp those hundreds
    of bucks were puked—

A mere appetizer, that fish, hors-d'oeuvre
    in a modest feast.
This man's now chief of the knights,
    who once was only too pleased
To sell his Egyptian brothers, yelling,
    "Mudcats for sale!"

Begin, Calliope! Here's no lyric for   [34]
    song; a tale
That's true is to be the subject.
    Now let's take our seats.
Pierian maidens, recount the story.
    And in that I treat
You to the name of maiden, may I be
    profited.

When the last of the Flavians was flaying   [37]
    a world half dead,
And Rome was slave to a baldheaded
    Nero, there appeared
In a net in the Adriatic, before the
    shrine that's reared
To Venus high over Greek Ancona, a
    turbot whose size
Was gigantic. It bulged at the
    meshes—a fish as much a prize
As those the Sea of Azov hides under
    ice till the sun
Cracks open the crust, and sluggish
    but fat from cold, they run
To the rushing Black Sea's mouth.
    The skipper means this whale
Of a fish for the chief pontiff—for
    who'd dare put on sale
Or buy so big a fish when even the
    beaches were thick
With informers? Customs men, inspecting
    seaweed, would be quick

To dash off and charge the helpless
    fisher, with no qualms
At swearing the fish long fattened in
    Caesar's ponds, therefrom
Escaped, and must be returned to its
    former lord. If we come
To believe what's held by Armillatus
    or Palfurius,
Everything that swims, is delicious,
    rare, or curious,
In any ocean whatever, belongs to the
    royal purse.
So, lest it go to waste, it shall be
    a gift he confers.

[56]   By now unwholesome autumn was yielding
    to frost at last,
Malarial patients hoped for relief,
    and cold winter's blast
Kept the fish quite fresh. And yet
    he hurried as if the hot
South Wind were dogging his heels.
    And when he'd gone somewhat
Past the lake where Alba, though ruined,
    tends the Trojan flame
And prays in the smaller temple of
    Vesta, a crowd that came
In wonder blocked his passage a while;
    and as it withdrew,
The gates on easy hinges swung out;
    and the senators who
Were excluded stared at the fish that
    got in. And it was sped
To this son of Atreus. Then the man
    of Picenum said:
"Accept a fish far too big for a
    mortal's kitchen. Declare
This a festival day. Make haste to
    vomit all that rich fare

In your stomach and eat a turbot
    preserved for your own reign.
The fish itself desired to be caught."
    What could be more inane,
More barefaced? And yet King Rooster's
    comb began to rise
With delight; when his power's
    praised as equal to that in the skies,
There's nothing a godlike emperor can't
    believe of himself.
But no dish big enough for the fish
    could be found on any shelf!

So the chief advisers were called   [72]
    into council—men he hated,
Upon whose faces was spread the ashen
    fear created
By his great and dangerous friendship.
    The first to rush
At the steward's call, "Hurry up, he's
    waiting!" was Pegasus,
Pulling on a snatched-up robe; for
    recently he'd been
Appointed as bailiff over the stunned
    city. Back then,
What else would a prefect be? But
    he was the best of the lot,
The most just interpreter of the law,
    although he thought,
In even those vicious times, that
    justice should not be dealt
By swords. Then came delightful old
    Crispus, whose unexcelled
And gentle spirit was equalled by
    his eloquent speech.
What better adviser for the monarch
    of the whole reach
Of oceans, lands, and nations if
    only he had been free,

Under that scourge and plague, to
    condemn his brutality
And give good moral advice? But what's
    more dangerous to men
Than the ear of a tyrant, upon whose
    whim the fate of a friend
Who spoke of showers, the heat, the
    rainy spring, depends?
So he never swam against the tide,
    nor was he such
A citizen as could utter the freeborn
    thoughts that touched
His heart, or risk his life for truth.
    He lived in this way
Through many winters and on to his
    eightieth birthday,
Protected in even that court by weapons
    like these from harm.

[94]   Behind him hurried Acilius, a man the
    same age, at his arm
The son who did not deserve the cruel
    death in store,
So quickly rushed upon him by his
    ruler's swords.
But to be both old and noble has become
    long since
The same as being a prodigy; it follows,
    hence,
That I'd rather be a clod, baby
    brother of giants, than those.
It was no help, therefore, to his
    wretched son that in close
Combat, as a naked huntsman, he speared
    Numidian bears
In the Alban arena. For who would
    not nowadays be aware
Of patrician tricks? Who'd think that
    old-fashioned ruse you achieved,

Brutus, was wonderful? Kings wearing
    beards are easily deceived.

With no happier face, though of ignoble   [104]
    bloodlines, Rubrius came—
Condemned long ago of crime no one
    mentions, yet deeper in shame
Than a satire-writing pervert. Then
    appeared the gluttonous belly
Of Montanus, and slightly later
    Montanus himself; and smelly
Crispinus, exuding at early daybreak
    enough strong scent
To outsmell two funerals. More
    vicious than he, next went
Pompeius, who had a tender whisper
    that slit men's throats;
And Fuscus, who, planning wars in his
    marble halls, would devote
His guts to Romanian vultures.
    Cautious Veiento in turn
Arrived with lethal Catullus, who with
    passion burned
For a girl he'd never seen—in even
    our times a great
And notable marvel, a blind sycophant,
    a dread courtier straight
From the beggars' bridges, worthy to
    beg at chariot wheels
And blow soft kisses to those descending
    the Arician hill.
No one was more amazed at the fish,
    for he said a great deal
About it, turning left. But the
    creature lay to his right.
In the same way, he'd praise a Cilician
    gladiator's fight
Or the hoist that snatches boy actors
    up into the flies.

[123]   But Veiento will not be outdone. Like
        a seer who prophesies
When nipped, O Bellona, by your gadfly,
        in frenzy he cries:
"An omen divine you have here, of a
        brilliant, great victory!
You'll capture some barbarous king,
        or Prince Arviragus will be
Knocked out of his British car and die.
        This beast, I opine,
Is of foreign birth. For see you not
        along the spine
Those spearlike fins?" There was nothing
        left for Fabricius, then,
Except to mention the turbot's age
        and its origin.

[130]   "Then what's your advice?" the emperor
        asked. "Cut it in two?"
"Heaven forfend," said Montanus; "such
        indignity will not do!
Command a deep vessel to be molded,
        of size so immense
Its thin walls can fitly embrace his
        gigantic circumference.
For the dish a great and instant
        Prometheus must come!
Make haste with clay, with wheel!
        But henceforth, O Caesar, let some
Good potters always attend your camp."
        This proposal, suited
Well to the man, won out. The old
        dissipations rooted
Deep in the royal court he knew, and
        Nero's soirées
That lasted beyond midnight, till a
        second hunger was raised

Inside them, when the blood by Falernian
    wine was heated.
No one in my time had greater knowledge
    of eating than he did.
He knew at the first bite if an oyster
    was born on a bed
In the Lucrine Bay, on Campania's
    rocks, or had been sped
From Kent; a glance revealed the coast
    where a sea urchin was bred.

The session's adjourned and the   [144]
    councillors are sent outside
Whom the mighty monarch had dragged
    posthaste and terrified
To his Alban palace as though he'd
    give them news of fierce
Germanic tribes on the warpath, or
    there had come to his ears,
With the speed of carrier pigeons flown
    from the faraway
Outposts of the empire, some quite
    alarming communiqué.

Even so, if only he had devoted to   [150]
    trifling nonsense
Like this all those days of cruelty
    and violence
When he robbed the city of its most
    noble and brilliant souls,
Unpunished, with none to avenge!
    But once he began to hold
Great terror for men in the lower
    classes, he was killed,
Soaked in the noble Lamian blood
    that he had spilled.

V

dinner with a patron

If you're not yet ashamed of your
    purpose and your mind
Is unchanged in thinking the greatest
    good is being dined
At another's board, if you can suffer
    things that neither
Sarmentus nor cheap Gabba would have
    endured at Caesar's
Table, I'd be afraid to trust you
    on the stand
As witness, even on oath. I know
    nothing with simpler demands
Than the belly; but even supposing
    you lack the fare
To fill your empty stomach, can't you
    find somewhere
A corner, a bridge, a pier, and be
    a panhandler there?
Is a free meal worth the insults, your
    hunger so acute
That it wouldn't be more dignified,
    shivering and destitute,
To choke down molded scraps the dogs
    leave in garbage cans?

[12]   First of all, don't ever forget: when
        asked to dinner, a man's

Being paid in full for every service
    he gave long before.
A meal is the harvest of great
    friendship; the nabob scores
A debit against your account; and
    though you get but few,
Each dinner is charged anyway. So
    after a month or two,
If he wants to invite his client,
    neglected and long denied,
Lest the bottom place at the bottom
    table be unoccupied,
He says, "Let's get together." The
    height of bliss! What more
Can you want? Now Trebius gets the
    reward for which he bore
The need to cut sleep short and
    run with shoestrings untied,
For fear the whole mob of fawners
    already has gone inside,
At an hour when all the stars are
    fading in the sky
Or Boötes' cold oxcart is slowly
    wheeling by.

And what a dinner, after all! You're   [24]
    given a wine
That even a poultice would not take;
    and then you'll find
The guests turned into Corybants.
    They start with vile names,
And soon the cups are flying, a battle
    roars and flames
Between you and a band of freedmen,
    crockery cracks your head,
You swab your wounds with napkins,
    quickly turning blood red.
But your host drinks vintage wine,
    bottled when consuls wore

Long hair and beards. He holds a
    glass of this juice, before
The Social Wars pressed out, but not
    a sip would he think
To send to a friend who suffers
    heartburn. Tomorrow he'll drink
An Alban or Setian wine, whose date,
    district, and chateau
Are hidden by a thick mold that time has
    allowed to grow
On the aged jars. Thrasea and
    Helvidius used to raise
Such wine and drink "in their leafy
    crowns" on all birthdays
Of Cassius and the Bruti.

[37]   The cup that Virro displays
Is a golden one, thick studded with
    beryl, a goblet encrusted
With sun-drenched amber and gems.
    To you no gold is entrusted;
Or if perhaps it is, then a steward
    is placed on guard
To count the jewels and keep a sharp
    eye upon your sharp
Fingernails. But pardon his qualms—
    that splendid jasper is much
Admired. For Virro, like others,
    transfers from his fingers such
Fine gems as Aeneas, preferred to
    jealous Iarbas, used
To jewel the hilt of his sword, and
    in new cups has them fused.
But you—you'll drain a cracked
    four-nozzled cup that bears
A drunk cobbler's name, whose glass
    needs sulfur for repairs.

If his lordship's stomach burns from   [49]
    food and wine, they place
Before him water, boiled but cold as
    frost in Thrace.
Was I complaining just now that you
    weren't served the same wine?
You hangers-on don't even drink the
    same water! Some fine
Gaetulian stableboy will set a cup at
    your seat,
Or the rawboned hand of a Moor you'd
    much prefer not to meet
At midnight passing the tombs on the
    hilly Latin Way.
Your host is served by the flower of
    Asia, a youth you'd say
Was bought for a bigger sum than all
    the wealth those kings,
The warrior Tullus and Ancus, had;
    in short, he'd bring
A price not all the estates of Roman
    kings would exceed.
This being the case, when thirsty,
    look for your black Ganymede.
That boy who cost those thousands can't
    mix a drink for a plain
Poor man. But his youth, his beauty,
    justify his disdain.
When will he come near you? When does
    he hear you ask
For water, hot or cold? Indeed, to
    do any task
For old clients is beneath him; he's
    injured that you demand
Anything of him and that you recline
    while he must stand.
But all great houses have plenty of
    haughty slaves on hand.

And look with what a growl another
    one holds out bread
You can scarcely break, a hard lump
    of dough already spread
With mold, impervious to teeth and
    sure to crack your jaws.
A loaf made out of fine flour,
    snow-white and soft as gauze,
Is served your host. But remember
    to keep your hands away;
Keep respect for the bread tray alive!
    But imagine that you may
Be slightly wicked, there'll still
    be someone there to make
You drop it. "Will you please, you
    insolent guest, just take
From your proper tray and learn the
    color of your own bread?"
"No doubt," you think, "it was for this
    that I have fled
So often away from my wife and hurried
    up to the head
Of the chilly Esquiline Hill when
    spring skies rattled and broke
With savage hail and rain poured down
    in streams from my cloak?"

[80]   Look now at that mammoth lobster,
    with garnish of asparagus,
Being served your host—its breast,
    so plump and glorious
And bulging over the platter, borne
    high over you and your peers
By the tallest butler; look at that
    waving tail that sneers
Down on you guests. For you a shrimp
    is served in state—
One shrimp afloat on one half of one
    egg on a tiny plate—

An adequate meal for a graveyard
    ghost. He sloshes his fish
With Venafran olive oil; but that
    wilted salad, the dish
That's given you, poor thing, will
    smell of lamp oil, for what
Is poured on your plates was brought
    here by a sharp-prowed boat
From Numidia—such vile stuff that
    no one in Rome would dare
To go into the baths if an African
    king were there—
It will even keep you safe from
    snakebites anywhere.

Virro will get a mullet, one shipped   [92]
    from Corsican shores
Or Taormina's rocks, for our own sea
    has been drained by scores
Of mad gluttons; the fishmarket nets
    keep seining our coast and let
No Tyrrhenian fish mature. And so
    our kitchens get
Supplies from the provinces; from them
    comes the fish as well
That Laenas, the legacy hunter, buys
    and Aurelia resells.

A lamprey is served to Virro, the   [99]
    best the Sicilian Straits
Can present; for while South Wind
    confines himself and waits
In his prison home to dry his dripping
    wings, the vortex
Of Charybdis holds for rash fishnets
    no fear of wrecks.
For you an eel is waiting, some
    cousin of water snakes,

Or a pike speckled with ice-spots,
    a son of the Tiber that makes
Its way to the heart of Rome, as is
    its wont, by tours
Of underground vaults, and fattens
    on filth in the pouring sewers.

[107] I'd like a word with our host if
    he'll lend a willing ear:
"Nobody's asking such gifts as Seneca
    would volunteer
To his humble friends, or good Piso
    or Cotta used to bestow;
For the honor of giving was valued
    greater, long ago,
Than office or title. We only ask
    that at dinner you show
You are free and equal. Do this,
    and be like many men
Today—be rich just for yourself and
    poor to your friends."

[114] Before him the liver of a huge goose,
    a capon as great
As a goose, are set; and a boar,
    well worthy to feel the blade
Of blond Meleager, steams there.
    Then truffles will come, if spring
Be here and the hoped-for rain and
    thunderstorms may bring
This extra course. As the gourmet
    said: "Keep all your wheat,
O Libya; unyoke your oxen! Just send
    us truffles to eat!"

[120] While that goes on, lest any cause
    for offense be missing,

You may watch the carver caper and
    posture, with knife whizzing
Around, till he performs the whole
    dance his master prepared.
For it makes a mammoth difference
    with what gestures a hare
Or a hen is carved! But dare to
    speak one word at such meals,
As though you had three names, and
    you'll be dragged by the heels,
Like Cacus trounced by Hercules,
    and thrown out the door.
And when does Virro drink from one
    cup with you or, what's more,
Take one your lips have touched?
    Which of you is so reckless, so
Without shame, as to suggest to your
    host, "Let's drink"? Oh, no,
There are many things a man in a
    worn-out cloak daren't say.
But if some god or a godlike man,
    more kindly than fate,
Should give you the four hundred
    thousand of a knight, how great,
From being a nothing, how close a
    friend of Virro you'd be!
"Give Trebius this, serve Trebius
    that. Would you like for me
To cut you the loin, dear brother?"
    O money! To you he pays
This honor; *you* are his brother.
    Nevertheless, in case
You wish to be a great lord and prince
    of great lords, let
No little Aeneas play in your halls
    or, sweeter yet
Than he, no daughter; nothing will
    make your friend more dear
And delightful to you than a barren
    wife. But as it is here,

Though your Mycale should bear and all
    at once should pour
Three boys on their father's lap, Virro
    will be charmed and adore
The squalling brood and, when these
    infant parasites
Come to his table, will order little
    green smocks brought right
Away, and peanuts and pennies if those
    are what they request.

[146] Suspicious toadstools will be served
    to the lowly guests;
To the master, a mushroom such as
    Claudius ate before
That one his wife prepared, after
    which he ate nothing more.
Virro will order to be brought in to
    himself and to
The other Virros fruits whose scent
    alone would do
For a feast—such as in unending
    Phaeacian autumns grew,
Or which you'd think were robbed from the
    Hesperides. But you
Get a rotten apple like those gnawed
    by a monkey, equipped
With shield and helmet, who learns
    in fear of being whipped
To hurl, from the back of a shaggy
    goat, a tiny spear.

[156] You may perhaps think Virro begrudges
    the cost. Never fear!
He does this to make you suffer.
    For what mime play is more fun,
What comedy, than a grumbling belly?
    So all this is done,

In case you don't know it, to compel
    you to pour out tears
Of rage and grind your squeaking
    teeth too long. You appear
To yourself as a free man, a tycoon's
    guest; he thinks you—
Not bad guesswork—a slave to his
    kitchen's odor. For who
Could be so destitute as to suffer
    this patron twice
If as a boy he had worn the free man's
    golden device,
Or even the leather boss, the badge
    poor folk would wear?
The hope to dine well deceives you:
    "Look, that half-eaten hare
He'll give us now, or from the haunch
    of boar some bits;
We'll get what's left of the capon
    soon." So all of you sit
In silence, ready, with bread held
    tight, untasted, and wait.
It's a wise man who treats you thus.
    If you can tolerate
All this, you deserve it. Some day
    you'll offer, with shaven pate,
Your head to be slapped and won't
    be afraid of being skinned
By keen whips, worthy at last of such
    feasts and such a friend.

VI

why marry?
a gallery of women

In Saturn's time, I believe that
    Chastity lingered still
On earth, and could be seen for a
    while, when only chill
Caves offered meager homes and enclosed
    beneath one broad
And common shelter the fire, the
    herds, the household gods,
And all the family; when the hill-bred
    wife would spread
A mattress of boughs with leaves and
    straw and cover the bed
With skins of animals caught nearby—
    not a bit like you,
O Cynthia, nor like you who with
    tears clouded up your two
Bright eyes at the death of a sparrow,
    but a woman who bore
Her breasts to suckle burly babes
    and often was more
Unkempt than her husband, belching
    from acorn diets. Back then,
When the globe of earth was young and
    skies were new, the men
Who, born of splintered oaks or
    fashioned out of clay,

Had no real parents, lived otherwise.
    Perhaps in the day
Of Jupiter many traces of ancient
    Modesty
Survived—at least a few—but Jupiter
    couldn't see
His beard as yet, the Greeks as yet
    weren't ready to swear
By another's head, and no one feared
    that a thief would dare
To steal his greens or fruit, and he
    lived without a wall
Around his garden. Then, by slow
    degrees, from us all
Astrea withdrew to heaven, with
    Chastity at her side
As comrade, and the two sisters
    together took their flight.

An ancient, long-practiced custom,   [21]
    Postumus, is making the bed
Of another man shake and scorning
    the spirit at the head
Of the consecrated couch. In time
    every other sin
Was brought forth by the Age of Iron;
    but it was in
The Silver Age that the first adulterers
    were seen.
And yet, in times like ours, you're
    seeking a license and mean
To contract a marriage; already a
    master barber you bring
To dress your hair and perhaps you've
    already bought the ring.
You once had your wits about you,
    Postumus; but now you think
Of taking a wife? What Fury, what
    serpents, are driving you mad?

Can you let a termagant boss you when
    rope is so easily had
And so many windows open on dizzy
    leaps and the height
Of the Aemilian bridge so handy?
    If none of these modes of flight
Is to your taste, don't you think it
    might be better to take
Some boy as bedmate, who'd never
    quarrel all night, or make
You promise gifts as you twine, or
    complain if you resist
His pleas and sleep, instead of panting,
    and leave him unkissed?

[38]   But Ursidius likes the Julian law of
    marriage, intends
To bring up a sweet little heir and
    thereby miss being sent
Fat squabs and bearded mullets and
    all that the markets purvey
To legacy hunters. What can you call
    impossible today
If any woman would marry our Ursidius?
    If he—
For so long our most notorious man
    of adultery,
So often hidden, to save his
    skin, in a closet—sticks out
His silly head for the marriage
    yoke? And what about
His seeking a wife with old-time
    morals! O doctors, come lance
His too full-blooded veins! What a
    card! If ever you chance
To find a modest woman, prostrate
    yourself at the door
Of Jupiter's shrine, sacrifice a
    gilt-horned heifer before

Juno. So very few are the wives who
    are worthy to touch
The fillets of Ceres, few whose fathers
    are not very much
Afraid of their kisses. Weave a
    garland that will span
Your threshold, hang ivy thick on the
    door! But will one man
Be enough for Hiberina! You'll
    sooner force her to be
Content with just one eye! And yet
    you're telling me
Of the good repute of a girl who lives
    on her father's farm:
Well, let her live in Gabii, in Fidenae,
    without harm
As she lived in the country, and I'll
    believe your farmyard tale.
But who will assert that nothing
    happened in mountain vales
Or deep in caves? Have Jove and Mars
    now grown so old?

Do our colonnades show you one woman   [60]
    worthy to be told
Your vows? Do all the rows of all
    our theaters hold
One girl you could single out and
    love with confidence?
When girlish Bathyllus dances and
    in mime presents
The gestures of Leda, Tuccia can't
    hold back her bladder;
Apula suddenly whinnies with passion,
    as though a man had her
In his arms; and rustic Thymele
    watches and learns what's what.

[67] But when stage sets are stored,
    the theaters empty and shut
And only courtrooms resound and
    it's empty months before
The Megalesian Games, other people
    who are bored
Find relief in amateur plays, the
    thyrsus, mask, and tights
Of Accius. Urbicus, in an Atellane
    farce, excites
A laugh by Autonoë's gestures—and
    Aelia, who hasn't a cent,
Loves him! Some women pay high prices
    to open the vent
At an actor's crotch, while others
    won't let Chrysogonus sing,
And Hispulla simply adores tragedians;
    but do you think
That any would love Quintilian? You
    take a wife, and take
A long chance the harpist Echion or
    Glaphyrus won't make
You a father—even Ambrosius, the
    flute player. Array
The bleachers along your narrow street,
    hang wreaths of bay
On doors and gates, that your noble
    heir, Lentulus, may
In his tortoise cradle exhibit far
    less resemblance to pater
Than to husky Euryalus or some other
    gladiator.

[82] When Eppia, a senator's wife, ran off
    with such an athlete
To Pharos, the Nile, and the infamous
    walls of Lagus, that seat
Of vice, Canopus, condemned the
    monstrous way of our city.

Forgetful of home, of husband and
    sister, devoid of pity,
She thought not of her country and
    left, unmoved by shame,
Her weeping children and even—more
    to amaze you—the games
And that actor Paris. Though born
    to wealth, though she had slept
As a baby on paternal goose down in a
    cradle swept
With lace, she scoffed at the sea
    just as she long had scoffed
At a good reputation, the loss of which
    is the least of our soft
Chair-riding ladies' concern. And
    so with good heart and no loss
Of courage she bore the roaring
    Tyrrhenian Sea, the toss
Of Ionian and all the other seas she
    had to cross.
A woman, if faced with danger for
    just and honest cause,
Is afraid, her breast with terror
    freezes, her legs are straws,
Trembling, and won't support her.
    But if she's doing a bold
And wicked thing, her courage never
    fails. To be told
By her husband to board a ship is
    cruelty; she gets sick
From the smell of bilge and rocking
    skies. But firm as a brick
Is her stomach if she's eloping with
    a lecher. She'd vomit
All over her husband if he were there,
    but now, far from it,
She eats with the crew, strides down
    the deck, and even enjoys
Hauling and coiling rough wet ropes
    with the sailor boys.

[103] Then what youth captivated Eppia, what
        beauty set her aflame?
What did she see in him to make her
        endure the name
Of "Madame Gladiator"? For it wasn't
        just yesterday
Dear Sergius began to shave or, with
        an arm wounded, say
He hoped to retire. And further,
        many blemishes showed
On his face, like welts from helmets,
        a huge wart on his nose
At the tip, and a foul rheum always
        seeping from his eyes.
All the same, a gladiator—a name
        that transforms those guys
Into Hyacinthuses! She put such a
        creature above
Her children, country, sister, and
        husband. What they love
Is the sword! And this same Sergius,
        when his release occurred,
Would have begun to seem like some
        Veiento to her.

[114] But do you care what a private
        household did, or what
This Eppia did? Then look at the
        rivals of the gods
And hear what Claudius bore: When
        his wife knew he was asleep,
This imperial harlot, without a trace
        of shame, would creep
From the marriage bed in the palace
        to seek the pallet of lust
That she preferred. Clad in a
        night cloak, she left with just

One maid, and with black hair disguised
　　by a blond wig, served
In a brothel where an empty crib was
　　always reserved
For her, with sheets still reeking
　　from the last encounter.
There she stood in the door, waiting
　　for men to mount her,
Naked, with nipples gold-tipped,
　　and Lycisca as business name,
And flaunted the womb whence you, O
　　noble Britannicus, came.
She welcomed all comers warmly, and
　　always demanded her pay.
At dawn, when the bawd dismissed his
　　girls, she chose to stay,
The last to close her stall; and
　　still with fire in her womb,
Erect like a man in her heat, she sadly
　　left the room.
Exhausted by dozens of men but still
　　not satisfied,
With sweaty cheeks, begrimed with
　　the smoke of lamps, now dried,
She brought to the palace bed a
　　perfect whorehouse stench.
Why talk of love potions, spells,
　　or poisons brewed to quench
A stepson's life? These sex-mad,
　　sex-driven women don't wince
At doing the foulest crimes; and
　　lust is the least of their sins.

"But why is Censennia the best of　　　[136]
　　wives, as her husband swears?"
Her dowry was in the millions; at a
　　price so right, he declares
Her chaste. He never lost weight
　　from Venus's darts, nor burned

From her torch: that dowry lit his
  fire, shot the arrows. In turn,
For her it bought liberty. She may
  flirt before his eyes
And write love letters; the wealthy
  wife of a man who sighs
For nothing but money is really
  unmarried in any case.

[142] "Why does Sertorius burn with love
  for Bibula?" Chase
The truth down and you'll find it's
  not the wife but the face
He loves. Let just three wrinkles
  appear, or let her skin
Get dry and flabby, her teeth turn
  dark, her eyes begin
To lose their luster, his freedman
  will say, "Pack up your clothes
And go! You're now a nuisance, always
  blowing your nose.
Get out, in a hurry! Another's
  coming whose nose doesn't run."
Till then she's queen, all afire,
  beseeching her husband at once
For shepherds, Canusian sheep,
  Falernian vineyards—mere
Trifles to start with—then all his
  slave boys and entire
Prison gangs. And what a neighbor
  has that she doesn't own,
He must buy. In the winter months,
  when the merchant Jason, shown
In a picture, is hidden and his
  armed sailors on the walls
Of the market are shut off during
  the fair by canvas stalls,
She brings home big crystal vases,
  bigger ones carved of myrrh,

And at last a famous diamond, made
    more precious to her
By the finger of Berenice. Long ago
    the barbarian king
Agrippa gave to his incestuous
    sister this ring
In that land where kings go barefoot
    on the Sabbath to hold
The rites, and pigs by ancient mercy
    are left to grow old.

"Not one from all these crowds strikes   [161]
    you as worthy to wed?"
Let her be beautiful, gracious, wealthy,
    fertile, and spread
Noble ancestors through her halls,
    let her be more chaste by far
Than any disheveled Sabine maid who
    stopped the war,
Indeed a rare bird on this earth, as rare
    as is a black swan.
But who could endure a wife who had
    all the virtues known?
I'd much rather have a wife used to
    rural ways, than you,
Cornelia, mother of the Gracchi, if
    with your true
Great virtues you bring a haughty
    pride and count with these,
As part of your dowry, your father's
    triumphs. I beg you, please,
Spare me your Hannibal, spare me your
    Syphax who fell
In his own camp—may all of Carthage
    and you go to hell!

"Have mercy, Apollo, I pray!   [172]
    O Goddess, pray lay aside

Your arrows! My children did nothing!
    Shoot their mother!" cried
Amphion. But Apollo drew his bow.
    So Niobe doomed
Her troop of offspring, even their
    father, when she presumed
To be nobler than Latona in
    progeny and to be
More prolific than the white sow of
    Alba. What dignity,
What beauty, in a wife are worth the
    price if she's
Forever reckoning up her virtues to
    you? For these
Supreme and rarest qualities lose
    their charm and pall
When spoiled by a pride formed less
    of honey than of gall.
And who is so deeply in love he never
    shrinks at all
From the very woman he praises to the
    skies—what's more,
Hates her at least sixteen hours out
    of the twenty-four?

[184] Some faults are small indeed, yet
    more than husbands can bear.
What's more disgusting than to find
    no woman will dare
Believe she's lovely unless converted
    from Tuscan to Greek,
From a girl of Sulmo to Maid of
    Athens? They can't even speak
Good Latin, more's the disgrace, and
    yet they talk a blue streak
All day long in Greek. They pour
    out their troubles, anger, fear,
Joys, and soul secrets in this lingo.
    What more would you hear?

All right—they're sleeping with men
    in Greek! You might permit
This in young girls; but when you're
    pushing eighty-six,
Must you still babble Greek? This
    tongue's not decent when heard
From an aged woman. When you utter
    such wanton words
As *Zoe kai Psyche* for "Life and Soul,"
    you're using speech
In public that should be under bedclothes.
    For how they beseech
And rouse the organs of lust—those
    soft wicked words! They caress!
Though you say them more sweetly than
    Haemus or Carpophorus,
You'll make all his ardent feathers
    fall, nevertheless—
Your age is computed by the wrinkles
    upon your face.

If you don't intend to love the woman   [200]
    you embrace
And marry in legal form, there seems
    no reason for you
To marry, no reason why you should
    waste the supper and new
Wedding cakes that must be given to
    well-stuffed guests who leave
When the party's over, or waste the
    gift of the bridal eve,
The rich tray gleaming with coins
    engraved with victories
In Dacia and Germany. If you simply
    must appease
Yourself with a wife and are devoted
    to one, incline
Your head, submit your neck to the
    marriage yoke. You'll find

No woman who spares the man who loves
    her. Though she glow
With passion, she loves to torment
    and plunder her lover. So,
The more he's good and desirable as
    a husband, the less
Beneficial by far will be his wife.
    You'll never address
A gift if she says no, never sell
    things if she objects,
Never buy anything unless she consents.
    And she will select
Your friends for you and turn your now
    aged friend from the door
That saw his beard first sprouting.
    Although the entire corps
Of pimps and trainers are free to draw
    up wills as they please,
And gladiators have the same right,
    your helpmeet sees
That you list as heirs more than one
    rival of your own.

[219] "Crucify that slave!" "For what
    crime does he deserve to atone
By death? What witness is there?
    Who accused him? Let him make
A defense. No delay's too long
    when a man's life is at stake."
"You idiot, you call a slave a man?
    He did nothing—agreed!
But this is my will, my command.
    Let my will justify the deed."
Thus is she lord of her lord. But
    before long she abdicates
Her throne and flies from bed to bed,
    and at this rate
Wears out her bridal veil; then she
    runs back to the bed

She scorned and seeks her imprint on
    it. The house she just fled
Is newly adorned, with bridal wreaths
    still green on the wall.
So grows her score in husbands; the
    limit of eight is her haul
In five autumns—a thing that merits
    a tribute on her tomb!

You'll have to despair of knowing   [231]
    any peace at home
If your mother-in-law's alive. She
    teaches your wife to delight
In stripping you of wealth, she
    teaches her how to write
Replies, in a style not crude or naïve,
    to the billets-doux
Of seducers, and she eludes or bribes
    your retinue
Of guards. She summons Dr. Archigenes,
    although
Your wife is well, and throws off the
    heavy covers so
The lover, meanwhile hid in a closet,
    may see but must wait
In silence, impatient at the delay,
    and masturbate.
But really, do you expect that a
    mother would hand down
To her daughter honest ways, which
    are opposite to her own?
Of course not—a vile old whore
    continues to profit by proxy
In rearing her darling daughter to
    be an expert doxy.

There's hardly a case in court that   [242]
    a woman's fuss didn't start.

If Manilia's not the defendant, she's
    the plaintiff. She'll chart
The suit herself, write briefs,
    answer charges, be ready to teach
Even Celsus to argue his case and
    strengthen his jury speech.

[246] Who doesn't know women who use the
    athlete's rubdown oils
And wear fine purple sweatcoats?
    Who hasn't seen one with foils,
Stabbing away at a post, lunging with
    shields and shrieks,
And piercing it to the heart, all
    with proper techniques?
She's well qualified to blow a
    trumpet in Flora's games,
Unless in her heart she considers
    something beyond and trains
For the real arena. What modesty
    can a woman show
Who wears a helmet and disowns her
    sex? She loves to go
Into manly pursuits; but even she
    wouldn't choose to be male,
For how paltry are the pleasures of
    us men! At a sale,
What honor a husband feels with his
    wife's athletic gear,
Sword belts, gauntlets, shinguards,
    put up by an auctioneer!
Or if she leans to a different sort
    of battle, you'll see—
Lucky you!—your young wife selling
    a whole fighting armory.
These are the girls who sweat in the
    thinnest of gauzy gowns,
Whose delicate flesh burns even in
    silk. But notice her sounds

Of grunts and roars as she thrusts a
    sword, see how she bends
At a helmet's weight, how coarse and
    thick the pads that defend
Her thighs! But when at last she
    drops her armor, then
You can laugh, for there is one male
    weapon she hasn't got—
No use in her standing up, she has
    to squat on the pot.
O daughters of ancient statesmen,
    of Lepidus, of the blind
Metellus or Fabius Gurges, what
    gladiator's wife could you find
Who ever wore such equipment or
    panted to vanquish a post?

The bed where a wife lies never is free   [268]
    of complaints and a host
Of quarrels back and forth. There'll
    be little sleep in that bed.
There she assails her husband, worse
    than a tigress is said
To be at the loss of her cubs. Aware
    of her own secret deeds,
She pretends to grieve, denounces
    the boys he's known, and weeps
At some feigned mistress, always with
    floods of tears at hand
Ever ready at their station, waiting
    for her command
On how they should flow. You think,
    poor worm, it's love they show,
Are pleased and kiss them away. What
    notes, what love letters, though,
There'd be to read if you opened the
    desk of your jealous whore!
Just catch her in the arms of a slave
    or knight, she'll implore,

"Tell me, tell me, Quintilian, the
    best words for my defense!"
"Beats me," he says; "think of some
    yourself." She says, "Long hence
It was agreed between us that you'd
    go your way and I'd
Go mine. You can deafen heaven and
    earth with bellows of pride—
I'm a human being." There's nothing
    bolder than women caught
Red-handed; out of their guilt their
    rage and courage are drawn.

[286] Where do these monsters come from,
    you ask; what's their source?
Long ago the humble state of the wives
    of Latium forced
Them to be chaste. Long hours of
    toil, short hours of sleep,
Hands chafed and calloused by Tuscan
    wool, the closer sweep
Of Hannibal toward the city, husbands
    on guard for Rome
On the Colline tower, kept vice from
    polluting the modest home.
Now we suffer the woes of long peace.
    Luxury, more savage
Than war, has smothered us, avenging
    the world we ravage.
From the day when Roman poverty
    vanished, we've lacked no crime,
No deed of lust. And so, to our
    Seven Hills from that time
The men of Sybaris, Rhodes, and Miletus
    have flowed, and among
The lot, the men of Tarentum, garlanded,
    wanton, and drunk.
Foreign ways were first brought in
    by filthy lucre, the health

Of the ages was sapped with vile
    indulgence by soft wealth.
For what does Venus care, when she's
    drunk? She doesn't know
Her head from her tail, at midnight
    slurps huge oysters, throws
Into her straight Falernian wine a
    frothing perfume,
And drinks it from a shell until the
    walls of the room
Spin dizzily, tables swim, and each
    light looks like a pair.

Come now, you wonder why Tullia   [306]
    with puckered face sniffs the air,
What Maura says in her vile Moorish
    foster sister's ear
When they pass the ancient shrine
    of Chastity? It's here
They stop their litters at night and
    piss on the goddess' form,
Squirting like siphons, and ride each
    other like horses, warm
And excited, with only the moon as
    witness. Then home they fly.
And you, setting out to greet fine
    friends with dawn in the sky,
Will tread on the traces of your
    wife's urine as you go by.

The secret rites of the Good Goddess   [314]
    are pretty well known,
When a flute stirs their loins and
    the Maenads of Priapus groan
And howl in frenzy from music and
    wine and toss their hair.
Oh, how they burn for intercourse,
    what cries declare

Their throbbing lust, how wet their
        legs with streaming juices!
Saufeia challenges the pimps'
        slave girls and produces
Such bouncing hips she wins the prize,
        but in turn must yield;
Medullina's copious flow is sure to
        carry the field.
The women share honors: technique's
        as good as breeding at this.
They're not pretending, as in a game,
        and each caress
Is genuine, such as would heat a
        Priam's cold blood and fire
A Nestor's testicles. Then impatient
        with chafing desire,
They're females without veneer, and
        around the ritual den
Rings a cry from every corner: "We're
        ready! Bring in the men!"
And if the stud is sleeping, the
        young man's ordered to wrap
Himself in a robe and hurry over.
        If he's not on tap,
A raid is made on the slaves; remove
        the hope of a slave,
They'll hire a water carrier. If
        they can't find a man, to save
The day they'll get a donkey to
        straddle their itchy behinds.
Oh, would that our ancient rites,
        at least in public shrines,
Were purged of these filthy acts!
        But every Hindu and Moor
Knows who that lady lute player was
        who, so cocksure,
Took a penis bigger than both the
        scrolls that Caesar wrote
Against Cato into a place that boy mice,
        taking note

Of their own testicles, flee; where
    every picture of males,
That opposite sex, is ordered covered
    well with veils.

Back then, who held the gods in   [342]
    contempt? Who would have dared
To laugh at Numa's wood bowls, black
    plates, and the brittle ware
Made out of Vatican clay? But now,
    what altar is there
Without its Clodius? * Females, high
    or low, have the same lust,
And she whose feet pound the black
    cobblestones is no better at best
Than she whose litter the shoulders
    of sturdy Syrians bear.

Ogulnia, in order to see the games,   [352]
    rents clothes, hires a chair
And porters, cushions, girl friends,
    a nurse, and a flaxen maid
To run errands. Yet what's left of
    the family silver plate,
Down to the last little mug, she
    gives to smooth athletes.
Many women have narrow means, but
    none is modest or meets
The fact of her poverty or limits
    herself to the budget
It allows and requires. But men look
    ahead sometimes and judge it
Wise to be thrifty; some at last
    have learned from the ant

* Three lines, 346–348, are in most texts at this point but
are obviously not in proper sequence. Since they occur below
in 0 29–34 in a logical sequence, I have omitted them here.

To fear cold and hunger. But when
a woman's extravagant,
She can't see that her funds are
dwindling. As though money grew
On trees to fill her empty coffers
and she well knew
A plentiful heap lay there, which she
could not exhaust,

[365] She never gives a thought to what her
pleasures cost.

[0 1] In any home where there lives and
disports a man avowed
To obscene affairs, his tremulous
fingers are endowed
With promise of everything. You'll
find they're all reprobate
And just the same as queers. But
folks let them desecrate
Their food and sit at their sacred
board, and when at last
Some Colocyntha or bearded Chelidon
ends his repast,
They order the dishes taken out to
be washed instead
Of having them smashed to pieces.
So even the lowborn head
Of a school for gladiators runs a
more decent house
Than yours; he keeps the foul and
the clean apart, allows
Not even net casters to mix with men
whose robes show dirt;
And armored fighters don't strip in
the same room with experts
At the trident, who always battle
naked. He never fails

102

To allot these guys the remotest
    quarters, and even jails
Do the same. And yet your wife makes
    you share the cup they use,
With whom a whore, decayed and brown
    as a corpse, would refuse
To drink the finest of wines. By
    their advice, on a whim
Impulsive women marry and get divorced;
    with them
They lighten boredom and business
    matters; from them they learn
To twitch their buttocks and thighs
    and whatever other turn
The teacher knows. But you must never
    trust him at all:
He mascaras his eyes, and decked in
    a yellow frock, net shawl
Tied round his hair, he aims at
    adultery. Don't fall
For his trick; the more he lisps, the
    more often his hands are spread
On his prissy hips, suspect him.
    He'll be a he-man in bed.
There he drops the mask of soft Thaïs
    and proves in fact
A three-pronged threat. "Whom are
    you fooling? Try your act
On other folks, not me. I'll make
    you a bet. I contend
You're a genuine man. Do you admit
    it? Or must I depend
On the tortured girls in brothels to
    tell?" I know the course,
Old friends, that you advise: "Put
    a lock on, keep her indoors."
But who's to guard the guards themselves?
    For pay in kind,
Their lips are sealed on the wanton's
    intrigues. As partners in crime,

[0 34] They're silent. A smart wife sees to
    this and begins with them.

[366] Those timorous eunuchs without one
    hope of a beard to trim
  Delight some women with luscious kisses,
    and there's no need
For abortives. The acme of bliss for
    such a woman, indeed,
Is one who was still a lusty youth,
    his private parts
Mature in a nest of hair, when
    remodeled by surgical arts.
Anyway, what's left grows bigger and
    soon weighs a goodly amount;
What the surgeon cut out makes a loss
    to only the barber's account.
But slave dealers' boys burn
    with a real and wretched disease
Of impotence, ashamed of the
    pouch and its lost chick-peas.
And when he goes to the baths—the
    other one caught in youth—
All eyes in admiration observe him,
    for in plain truth
He rivals Priapus, though his mistress
    had him castrated.
Let him sleep with her; but keep this
    eunuch well separated,
Postumus, from sturdy Bromius, who's
    barely ready to shave!

[379] If your wife loves music, no professional
    singer can save
  Himself from her summons. She's always
    handling instruments;

Her sardonyxes sparkle all over the
    lyre as she invents
A group of chords with a vibrating
    plectrum formerly used
By tender Hedymeles. This trophy she
    fondles, and suffused
With delight, she washes his pick with
    kisses and teary brine.
A certain lady, of Lamian and Appian
    blood, with wine
And cakes asked Janus and Vesta if
    Pollio might aspire
To the Capitoline oak wreath and
    promise it to his lyre.
What more could she have done if her
    husband were ill, her son
Despaired of by the doctors? She
    stood at the shrine and not one
Vestige of shame did she feel to veil
    her head and pray
For a harpist, spoke the prescribed
    words in the proper way,
And paled when the lamb was opened.
    Tell me, I ask you now,
Most ancient of gods, O Father Janus,
    do you allow
Such women answers? You've time on
    your hands in heaven; for you,
You gods, so far as I can see, there's
    nothing to do.
One lady consults you about a comic
    actor; again,
Another wants to commend a tragedian.
    Soon, for their pains
In serving so much, soothsayers will
    all have varicose veins.

But better that she should sing than   [398]
    boldly rush around

The whole city, intrude on the
    councils of men, and talk down,
Straight-faced, dry-bosomed, the
    leaders in military clothes,
In front of her husband. This same
    woman knows what goes
On all around the world—what the
    Russians and Chinese propose
To do, down to what wife did what
    with her stepson and where.
She knows who loves whom, what wolf's
    the rage, what widow will bear
A babe, who did it and when. She'll
    tell you what women cry
To lovers in bed, and how they do it.
    She's first to spy
The comet threatening kings of Armenia
    and Parthia, first
To pick up the latest rumors
    at the gates, and well versed
At inventing them. So she tells
    everyone on every corner:
Earthquakes have leveled distant
    cities, the great Matterhorn or
Gibraltar has burst its banks, is
    flooding the land, the blight
Spreads miles all around, whole regions
    are sinking from sight!

[413] This fault is bad, but no worse to
    bear than a woman who
Always grabs up poor neighbors and,
    though for mercy they sue,
Cuts them with whips. If her sleep
    is ruined by a barking dog,
She cries, "Get the canes! Be quick!"
    and gives an order to flog
The owner first and then the dog.
    Unpleasant to meet,

A most horrible face! She goes to
    the baths at night, when streets
Are dark, sends over her oil flasks
    and whatever's required.
She loves to sweat in the swarming
    crowd, and when she's tired
From swinging dumbbells, the cunning
    masseur must rub her with oil.
His fingers stray deeper into her
    brush until her loins boil
To a climax amid her cries. And
    meanwhile, back at her house,
Poor guests, half dead with fatigue
    and hunger, start to drowse.
At last she arrives, all red in the
    face and with a thirst
That could drain the whole wine basket
    set at her feet. But first
She tosses down a couple of pints from
    it before
Her dinner, to rouse a huge appetite,
    and then she pours
It out, to slosh what's washed from
    her stomach onto the floor.
The flood runs over the marble pavement,
    the gold basin stinks
Of Falernian, for like a big snake
    trapped in a vat, she drinks
And vomits and drinks. With this
    her husband grows meanwhile
Nauseated, and by shutting his eyes,
    holds down his bile.

But worse is the woman who, no sooner   [434]
    than she sits
At dinner, praises Vergil, forgives
    dying Dido, pits
The poets against each other, and
    weighs Vergil on the scale

With Homer. Grammarians yield,
    rhetoricians are beaten, turn tail,
And the whole assemblage is silent.
    No lawyer, no auctioneer,
Can get a word in, nor even another
    woman. To hear
Such a pounding force of words, you'd
    think so many bells
And basins were being crashed together.
    It's just as well
That now no one should strain the
    trumpets and cymbals—one
Woman alone will be able to cure an eclipse
    of the moon.
The philosopheress sets rules and
    expounds on moral sense;
But she who yearns too much to seem
    wise, full of eloquence,
Should tuck her skirts up to her
    knees like a man, sacrifice
A pig to Silvanus, and go to cheap
    baths at a scholar's price.
Don't let the wife who shares your
    bed know polemical speech,
Don't let her badger you with twisted
    words and preach
In slyly distorted syllogisms. And
    let her not know
All the histories, but read some things
    in books, although
She doesn't understand them. I hate
    one who always
Consults and goes through Palaemon's
    grammar, in every phrase
Observing rules and usage of speech
    and who, in effect
An antiquary, quotes verses unknown
    to me and corrects
In her rustic girl friends errors no
    man need worry to make.

Let a husband at least be allowed his
    "grammatical" mistakes.

A woman stops at nothing, for nothing's   [457]
    shameful, she thinks,
When she rings her neck with emeralds
    and hangs to her ears gold links
With pearls big enough to stretch them.
    Nothing's so hard to endure
As a wealthy woman. Before that, her
    face is foul, each contour
Grotesquely puffed by beauty packs,
    and she reeks and drips
With thick Poppaean creams, which
    stick to her poor husband's lips.
A lover she greets with skin washed
    clean. But when will she care
To look attractive at home? For lovers,
    spikenard's kept there;
For them she buys all that you slender
    Hindus in commerce
Send us. At last she opens her face,
    strips off the first
Of the plasters, and begins to look
    recognizable; then
She's laved in asses' milk, from a herd
    of females, which in
Her train would be led if she were
    banished to the North Pole.
But when she's daubed and treated with
    all those creams and mole
Removers and wrinkle smoothers of
    hot, wet dough, the results are
Questionable: What shall we call it—
    a face or an ulcer?

It's worth while to learn exactly what   [474]
    they do all day

And how they keep themselves occupied.
    If a husband lay
Backed up to his wife at night,
    the housekeeper gets it, maids
Are stripped for the lash, the Liburnian
    chair-man she upbraids
For coming late, and *he* has to pay
    for the sleepy head
Of her husband. Canes are broken on
    one, another turns red
With blood from thongs, a third from
    whips. Some women hire
Their torturers by the year. The
    flogging starts, and while
It goes on, she daubs her face, or
    listens to her girl friends,
Or inspects the wide gold thread of
    embroidered robes. Again
The whip falls—she reads the
    Daily Gazette; again the whip scores,
Until at last, with the floggers
    themselves exhausted, she roars
A horrendous "Get out!" and her court
    of justice is adjourned.

[486] Her government of her own household
    is just as stern
As that of Sicilian tyrants. For if
    she's made a date
And wants to be prettier dressed
    than usual, and is late
And hurried to meet whoever waits
    for her in the park,
Or more likely the bawdy temple of
    Isis, then she'll bark
At the girl who does her hair—unhappy
    Psecas, with hair
In tangles, herself, with shoulders
    naked and bosom bare:

"Why is this curl much higher?"
    And so the bullhide thong
Chastises her for the fault of a curl.
    What did Psecas do wrong?
Is the girl to blame if you don't
    like the shape of your nose?
On the left, another maid combs her
    hair and coils it in rows.
A maid of her mother's, too old for
    sewing but now in charge
Of spinning, joins the council; she's
    the first to enlarge
On her views, and after her the younger,
    less skilled, will state
Their opinions, all as though honor
    or life were in debate:
So serious is the business of being
    beautified,
So many tiers she piles up, so many
    stories besides
She builds high on her head. An
    Andromache you'll see
In front; behind she's shorter; you
    wouldn't think it could be
The same woman. Well, maybe nature
    made her so short that she
Looks like a Pygmy maiden without the
    help of high heels,
And has to rise up lightly on tiptoe
    in order to steal
A kiss. Meanwhile, she gives no
    thought, much less any care,
To husband or what she costs. She
    acts, though living there,
As if she were his neighbor—closer
    only through hate
Of his friends, his slaves, and her
    wasting of his wealth.

[511]   In the gate
The priests of mad Bellona and Cybele
        come, led through
By a huge half-man, a form that his
        obscene minor crew
Must revere, who cut off his tender
        genitals long ago
With a broken shell. To him the
        noisy crowds bow low,
To him the drummers yield; a Phrygian
        turban adorns
His plebeian features. The lady in
        solemn tones he warns
Of September hurricanes coming, unless
        she will purify
Herself with a gift of a hundred eggs,
        and add a supply
Of old dark-red clothes, so that into
        them any sudden, severe
Forthcoming danger may pass and at
        once expiate the whole year.
On a winter morning she'll go to the
        river, break the ice,
Plunge into the Tiber, and dip her
        timorous head in it thrice,
In the eddies themselves; then, naked
        and shivering, crawl right
Across the whole Field of Mars on
        bleeding knees. If the white
Io commands it, she'll go to the ends
        of Egypt and fetch
From the Nile at tropic Meroë the
        sought-for water with which
To sprinkle Isis' temple that stands
        near the old sheepfolds.
For she thinks the voice of the goddess
        herself gave the word: what a soul,
What a mind, for the gods to be
        conversing with in the night!

Therefore the chief and highest honor
    is given by right
To Anubis who, surrounded by a
    linen-clad troop
And priests with shaven heads, runs
    along deriding the group
Of people bewailing Osiris. It's he
    who for pardon prays
Each time a wife won't abstain from
    copulation on days
That must be observed as holy, and
    huge penalties he takes
Whenever her sheets have been defiled,
    and the silver snake
Has been seen to nod its head. His
    tears and studied singsong
Make sure that Osiris won't deny pardon
    for the wrong,
Bribed, of course, by a thin holy
    cake and a big fat goose.

When he has taken his leave, a   [542]
    trembling Jewess, whose
Reed basket and hay are left behind,
    is begging her,
Whispering in her ear—this one's
    an interpreter
Of the laws of Jerusalem, high
    priestess with a tree
As temple, a trusty go-between of
    high heaven. And she
Fills her palm, but much less full, for
    at bargain prices a Jew
Sells you the answer to any dream
    you'd like to come true.

An Armenian or Commagenian soothsayer [548]
    next, who has picked

113

About in the lungs of a still-warm
    pigeon and now predicts
A youthful lover or a huge bequest
    from a man who's rich
And childless. He'll poke into chickens'
    hearts, the guts of a bitch,
Sometimes of babies. What he'd
    inform on, himself, he'll do.

[553] But she'll trust Chaldeans more.
    What astrologers construe,
They believe comes right from Ammon's
    mouth, for Delphi of late
Has no oracles and is mute, and man
    is condemned to wait
In darkness as to the future.
    Foremost among these was he,
So often exiled, through whose friendship
    and suborned augury
The great citizen, feared by Otho,
    died. Subsequently,
His art was trusted only if both hands
    had clanked with chains
And he in the prison house of a distant
    camp had lain:
No unconvicted astrologer has
    power—only he
Who, all but executed, contrived
    just in time to be
Exiled to the Cyclades and at last
    from Seriphos set free.

[565] Your Tanaquil consults them about the
    much delayed death
Of her jaundiced mother—earlier,
    though, about *your* last breath—
And when she'll bury her sister and
    uncles, and if she'll go

Before her lecher—what sweeter boon
    could the gods bestow?
But still she can't understand those
    gloomy, dreadful threats
Of the planet Saturn, or under what
    constellation she gets
The propitious influence of Venus,
    or which month is for gains,
Which month for losses. But remember
    the type—take pains
To avoid a woman who clutches a
    horoscope, well thumbed
In her hands, like a smooth amber
    ball, one who consults with none
But now herself is consulted, one who
    when her husband withdraws
To camp or returns to his home won't
    go with him because
The signs in Thrasyllus call her
    back. If she wants to ride
To the first milestone, the right
    hour is for her book to decide.
If the corner of an eye she rubbed
    should itch, she calls
For salve only after checking her
    horoscope; though she falls
Abed ill, no hour appears more proper
    for taking food
Than that which Petosiris has prescribed
    as good.

If she be of modest means, she'll   [582]
    shop around in each shed
Between the circus endposts, draw
    lots, let her palm be read,
Or have a phrenologist interpret her
    brow and head,
While asking many clucks of approval.
    Rich women get answers

From the highly paid Phrygian or
    Indian necromancers,
So skilled in stars and spheres,
    or some old priest whose role
Is to purge things hit by lightning.
    Plebeian fortunes are told
In the Circus or on the Servian ramparts.
    The woman who wears
A long chain of gold around her naked
    neck inquires
Before the pillars and dolphin columns
    if she should plan
On leaving the tavern keeper and
    wedding the old-clothes man.

[592] And yet, these impoverished women
    suffer the dangers and pains
Of childbirth and troubles of nursing,
    which their poor lot ordains.
But how few gilded beds contain a
    female sweating in labor!
It shows how fatal the skill, how
    potent the drugs, on babe or
Mother, when an abortionist gets high
    prices to kill
Mankind in the womb. Rejoice, poor
    husband; give her the pill
Or the dose yourself. For if she
    were willing to swell up and bother
Her womb with kicking babies, perhaps
    you'd be the father
Of an Ethiopian—and this dusky heir,
    whom you would hate
To meet before noon, would soon
    inherit your whole estate.

[602] I skip the substitute children,
    frauds that answer but cheat

Fond hopes and prayers. Abandoned
    beside cesspools, they meet
Our need for pontiffs and priests
    with bodies that falsely bear
The name of Scauri. Shameless
    Fortune always lurks there
In the night, smiling upon the naked
    babies; these
She fondles and wraps in her bosom;
    then, herself to please,
She prepares her private farce and
    sends them into the homes
Of the mighty. These she loves, to
    these her favors are shown;
She always brings them forth as
    nurslings of her own.

One man hawks magic charms for ladies,   [610]
    another sells
Love potions from Thessaly, which
    harass the mind with spells,
When a wife can spank her husband's
    rump with a shoe. They set
You to acting a fool, sow darkness
    in your mind—you forget
What you did last night. Yet all of
    that can be borne if you
Just don't begin to rave like that
    uncle of Nero's into
Whose drink Caesonia poured the whole
    afterbirth of a mare.
When an empress sets a style, what
    woman won't follow? Everywhere
The world was then in flames and
    falling, divided, to doom,
As if Juno had driven her husband mad.
    Agrippina's mushroom,
Therefore, was a lesser evil since
    that choked off the breath

Of just one old man and sent his
    doddering head in death
With slavering lips to descend to
    heaven; this other potion
Cried out for slaughter and fire, bred
    torture, mixed in an ocean
Of blood mutilated knights and senators.
    Such were
The costs of one mare's offspring and
    one female poisoner.

[627] They hate the children of their
    husbands' concubines.
Let none resent it, none forbid, now
    at last it's defined
As proper to kill a stepson. You
    orphan boys, whose wealth
Is in your own name, I warn—keep a
    close watch on your health,
Your life; don't trust one single
    dish. The meat pies are hot,
But also hot with a mother's poison.
    No matter what
The woman who bore you offers, let
    someone first take a taste;
Let your fearful tutor sip first from
    the cup set at your place.

[634] I'm inventing all this; my satire of
    course I have enlaced
In Tragedy's buskin? I've stepped
    out of bounds, broken the rules
Of those before me, drunkenly ranting,
    as if from the school
Of Sophocles, a dark theme our Roman
    mountains and skies
Never knew? I wish I were wrong!
    But here is Pontia who cries:

"I confess. I did it—poisoned my
    sons. My crime, laid bare,
Is known to all. With my own two
    hands I did it—so there!"
"You didn't, you fiendish viper,
    murder two at one meal?
Not two?" "Or seven, if seven by
    chance had been there to kill!"

Let us believe what Tragedy says of   [643]
    Procne and grim
Medea; I've no rebuttal. Those women
    dared in their time
Great monstrous deeds, but not on
    account of money; much less
Amazement is due the highest crimes
    when wrathfulness
Incites this sex to guilty acts, and
    blazing inside
With fury, they're swept headlong
    like rocks from ridges pried
When a mountain erodes and beetling
    crags crumble and split.
I can't bear a woman who plans and
    in cold blood commits
A terrible crime. Our wives watch
    Alcestis undergo
The fate of her husband; but if the
    gods on them should bestow
A similar chance of exchange, they'd
    let their husbands die
To save the life of a poodle dog.
    Each day you'll pass by
Granddaughters of Belus, many
    Eriphyles, and you can't miss
Clytemnestras in every street.
    The only difference is this:
That daughter of Tyndarus had to
    use both hands to swing

A clumsy two-headed ax, whereas nowadays
    the thing
Is done with toad poison. And yet,
    if Atrides, practicing
Precaution, has drunk beforehand the
    antidotes that healed
The thrice-conquered king of Pontus,
    it still is done with steel.

VII

the plight
of the creative man

All hopes and incentives of learned
    men lie in Caesar alone.
For in our time only he has regarded
    the Muses who moan
And grieve while famous poets must
    manage small baths in a place
Like Gabii, or bakeshops in Rome, and
    others have shown no trace
Of shame to become town criers; while
    starving Clio forsook
The valleys of Aganippe and came to
    town to look
For work. For if you see no chance
    to earn a cent
In the Muses' grove, you'd better
    decide to be content
With Machaera's name and profits,
    and sell what the auction match
Sells the crowd—wine jars, tripods,
    bookcases, chests, and a batch
Of Paccius' *Alcithoë* and Faustus'
    Tereus and *Thebes*. This tack
Is better than if you swore before a
    judge "I saw"
What you didn't see, though Asian
    knights may say this in law,

And knights of Bithynia and Cappadocia,
    too, and a breed
Like those whom Galatia brought across
    to us with bare feet.

[17]   But henceforth no man who weaves our
    eloquence into song
With musical meters and has bitten
    the laurel will long
Be forced to do labor beneath
    his talents. To work, young men!
Your emperor's looking around,
    urging you on that your pen
May produce a work he'll favor.
    But if you expect to find
A patron anywhere else, Telesinus,
    if with that in mind
You're scribbling reams of yellow
    paper, you'd better call
For firewood right now and sacrifice to
    Vulcan all
You write, or stop and let bookworms
    eat your book where it lies.
Break your pen in two, destroy the
    battles that kept your eyes
From sleep, poor fool, who go on
    writing verses sublime
In a tiny garret, expecting that you
    may merit in time
A scrawny bust with an ivy crown.
    There is no hope
Beyond that: our wealthy miser today
    has learned to cope—
Just admire, just praise the eloquent,
    like boys before
Juno's peacock. But that time of
    life, that could have borne
The sea or helmet or spade flows by;
    then fatigue imbues

The soul, and talented, paupered old
    age damns itself and its Muse.

Now hear the arts that spare him   [36]
    from spending anything
On you—that patron you're courting, after
    abandoning
The temples of the Muses and Apollo.
    He writes
Poems himself, and yields to Homer
    alone the heights
Of verse because of his thousand-year
    lead. And if you're ablaze
To recite, for the sweets of fame, he
    lends a moldering place
To you; this house in the suburbs is
    at your service, with doors
Of iron, like city gates repelling
    invaders. With scores
Of freedmen he fills the back rows
    and spreads his clients about
The room to cheer and applaud. But
    no rich man will put out
So much as the rent for benches,
    rostrum, steps, and chairs
In front, which have to be returned
    after these affairs.
But still we poets keep working and
    scratch our furrows now
In shallow dust and turn the sands
    with a profitless plow.
For if you'd stop, the incurable itch
    for writing holds
You in ambition's snare and in your
    sick heart grows old.

But a genuine poet, who has a personal   [53]
    lyric streak,

Who writes no hackneyed lines, whose
    verse is not, so to speak,
Coined in a common mint—this man,
    whom I cannot show
And only sense, is produced by a mind
    free of care, bearing no
Rancor, devoted to the forests, and
    worthy to drink
At the Muses' spring. For gloomy
    Poverty cannot think
Of singing in the Pierian cave, a
    thyrsus held tight
In hand, while having no money, which
    both day and night
The body needs. When Horace was
    singing, "Be merry," he kept
His belly well filled. Where can
    genius find a home except
In a heart moved only by song, to no
    other care inclined,
And urged by the lords of poetry and
    wine? An exalted mind—
Not one that quails at a blanket's
    cost—is needed to catch
A vision of chariots, horses, faces
    of gods, and to match
In verse what confounded Turnus—the
    sight of Alecto's face.
For if Vergil had lacked a slave and
    a decent dwelling place,
All of the snakes would have fallen
    out of her hair, no dire
Blast would have roared from her
    silent trumpet. Do we require
That Rubrenus Lappa be no less great
    than ancient playwrights,
When his *Atreus* lies in pawn for
    dishes and clothes? And quite
Unhappy Numitor has not a thing he
    can give a friend,

But enough for gifts to Quintilla,
    and some left over to spend
For a tame lion that must eat whole
    sides of beef. It costs less,
No doubt, to feed lions; poets have
    bigger bellies, I guess.

Lucan, content with fame, may rest   [79]
    among statues that grace
His gardens, but how will the greatest
    praise, if only praise,
Help Serranus or starving Saleius?
    Everyone flocks to hear
His lovely voice read their favorite
    Theban epic when dear
Statius has made the city happy by
    naming a day:
For so does he capture their hearts
    with music, so does he sway
The crowd to listen with rapture.
    But when his verses have brought
The house down, he'll starve unless
    he lets his *Agave* be bought,
Still virgin, by that actor, Paris.
    For he's the man
Who bestows many army commands, and
    rings with the golden band
Of a knight a poet's finger after six
    months. You'll get
From an actor more than princes give.
    Why haunt the rich set
Of the Camerini, of Barea, and the
    spacious halls
Of nobles? *Pelopea* chooses prefects,
    Philomela installs
Tribunes. But you really shouldn't
    begrudge the poet who
Earns a living from the stage.
    Who'll be a Maecenas to you?

Who'll be nowadays Proculeius or
    Fabius, who'll be
A second Cotta or Lentulus? Back
    then, ability
Was matched with reward, then it was
    worth it to many to try
To be pale and through December's
    revels let wine go by.

[98]   You historians, do you perhaps from
    all your work earn more?
You surely waste more time and more
    lamp oil on your chore.
Forgetting reason, your pages run
    into thousands—the cost
Of paper alone must ruin you! To
    this you're forced by the vast
Profusion of acts and by the laws of
    your craft. But what yield,
What harvest is got from it, what
    fruit from clearing your field?
Who'll give to any historian as high
    a rate of pay
As he will give the man who announces
    the news each day?

[105]   "They're a lazy bunch," you say,
    "that love just lying around
In the shade." Then what does a
    lawyer get, who in court expounds
His cases, loaded with bundles of
    briefs? He makes a big show,
Especially if his own creditors hear;
    indeed he will grow
Even louder if nudged by a man who's
    brought huge ledgers to claim
A dubious debt. His enormous bellows
    then pant as they frame

A big lie about his opponents, and
    all over his breast
He slobbers spit. And yet, if you
    really put to the test
His income, you'll balance a hundred
    lawyers' fees with what
A single redcoated jockey who races
    horses has got.
The judges are seated; you stand
    up, pallid as Ajax, to sue
In a case of contested freedom before
    some nincompoop who
Was made chief justice. Rant till
    you burst your lungs, poor fool,
And win for your pains green palms
    to adorn the vestibule
Of your attic home. And what's the
    fee for your speech? A butt
Of dry ham, a tin of sardines, five
    bottles of wine—rotgut
That came down the Tiber—or maybe
    a month's supply (for a Moor)
Of mildewed onions. If you've
    pled four times and procure
A gold piece, most of it, by your
    compact, goes to your clerks.
Aemilius will get top fees, though
    we did the better work.
But then, a chariot with four fine
    steeds in bronze appears
In his patio, and his own image,
    astride a fierce
Warhorse, is brandishing a slanted
    spear at a wide
Remove, and the statue practices
    for battle, squint-eyed.
For such things Pedo is bankrupt,
    Matho's broke, and the fate
Of Tongilius will be the same—
    he goes to the baths with a great

Oil flask of rhinoceros horn and
    irks everyone with his crowd
Of dirty slaves. He rides through
    the forum, with bearers bowed
By a king-sized litter, window
    shopping for slaves or vases
Of agate, silver or villas. His
    imported mantle places
Him high in the credit rating—it's
    Tyrian purple. Even so,
These people profit by this, for
    violet or purple robes throw
A lawyer more practice. To him it's
    worth it to live in a buzz
Of commotion and put on a show of
    having more than he does.
For prodigal Rome sets no limit on
    how much you squander, or how.

[139] Do we trust in eloquence? No one
    today would ever allow
Cicero himself the smallest fee unless
    he could show
A big blazing ring. The first thing
    a litigant has to know
Is: Have you eight slaves, ten
    flunkies, a litter; have you friends
In togas to walk before you? That's
    why Paulus used to rent
A sardonyx ring for his pleas in
    court, and why he earned
Higher fees than Gallus or Basilus.
    Seldom do people discern
Eloquence under a threadbare cloak.
    For when do they let
Basilus bring forth in court a
    weeping mother, or yet
Even listen, no matter how well he
    speaks? Much better to get

Out to Gaul or Africa, wet nurse of
    lawyers, if you are stung
With the thought of bringing in a
    living by use of your tongue.

But maybe you teach rhetoric? What   [150]
    an iron constitution
You must have, Vettius, to hear your
    full class plot executions
Of cruel tyrants! Whatever each
    pupil has read at his seat,
He'll stand to recite, and drone the
    very same lines that repeat
What others have said. This same
    warmed-over cabbage kills
The wretched teachers. What approach
    should be made, what bill
Of particulars for a case, what's
    the crucial point, and what
Will the main objections be, all
    wish to know, but wish not
To pay for. "Pay my tuition? But
    what did I learn?" It's the fault
Of the teacher, of course, that some
    Arcadian ass can't exalt
His feelings and harps on terrible
    Hannibal till my poor brain
By the weekend is numb with whatever
    it is he hopes to explain:
Whether to push toward Rome from the
    battle of Cannae, or whether
In caution, after the thunderstorms
    and threatening weather,
To wheel his troops, drenched from
    the rain. "Just name any sum
You please; you'll get it if you can
    make their fathers come
And hear them as often as I!" cry
    dozens of teachers as one,

Filing lawsuits for their pay, with
    real claims to argue—none
On "The Rapist," "The Poisoner,"
    or the others left behind
With "The Bad Ungrateful Husband" and
    "Miracle Drugs for the Blind."

[171] So if you want my advice, you men who
    come down from the shade
Of fictitious rhetoric to wage real
    battles in court to be paid
Your fees—worth a pauper's dole, but
    the best you'll ever receive—
To you I say, get out, give yourself
    walking papers, leave
For some other job. If only you
    knew how Chrysogonus clips
The upper crust for teaching their
    sons to sing, you'd rip
Your *Essentials of Rhetoric* by
    Theodorus right in two.

[178] A great man will spend ten thousand
    to build his baths, a few
More than that for a long colonnade
    to ride in on rainy days—
Must he wait for clear skies, or splash
    fresh mud on his team of bays?
Much better to drive where their hooves
    will stay unmuddied and bright!
Elsewhere let a banquet pavilion rise
    on pillars of white
Numidian marble and catch the winter
    sunlight. No matter
The cost of the house—he still can
    afford a slave for each platter,
To serve it with proper skill, and cooks to
    make tasty food.

Among such expenditures, two thousand
    is surely a good
Deal more than enough for Quintilian:
    There's nothing a father will spend
Less money on than his son. You ask,
    "How is it, then,
That Quintilian has so many estates?"
    Pass over the cases
Of unusual fortune; the lucky man
    is full of graces—
He's handsome, brave, and wise,
    highborn and noble; he sews
On his black shoes the Senate's half-moon;
    a great orator, too, he throws
The javelin for records, and even
    with a cold sings like a bird.
For it makes a big difference which
    stars welcome you when first
You start to utter squalls, still
    red from your mother's womb.
If Fortune chooses, you'll rise to
    consular post from classroom;
If she feels otherwise, you'll fall
    from consul to rhetor. For what
Was it that favored Ventidius? And
    Cicero? Was it aught
But the stars and the wondrous might
    of mysterious fate? They'll bestow
Kingdoms on slaves and triumphs on
    captives. Yet also,
That fortunate man is rare—more rare
    than a pure white crow.
Many men have regretted holding the
    vain, unrewarding chair
Of professor, as the end of
    Thrasymachus declares,
And of Secundus Carrinas; and him
    whom you saw low
In poverty, O Athens, on whom you
    dared bestow

No better thing than a cup of cold hemlock.
    Grant, O gods,
That earth lie soft on our forefathers'
    shades and through the clods
Eternal spring and the fragrant crocus
    bloom over their bones:
They honored a teacher as substitute
    parent. Even full grown,
Achilles, fearing the rod, used to
    sing in his native hills,
And the tail of the centaur, his
    music teacher, did not fill
Him then with laughter. But Rufus
    and other teachers today
Are beaten up by their own teen-agers—Rufus,
    whom they
Have nicknamed "Cicero from the sticks"
    so often before.

[215] Into the laps of Celadus or learned
    Palaemon, who pours
As much reward as their works of
    grammar deserve? And yet
From this, whatever it be—and it's
    less than rhetors get—
The pupil's pigheaded guardian takes
    his bite, and a cut
Must go to the steward. Accept it,
    Palaemon, and suffer somewhat
Of a loss in fees, like a peddler
    in winter with bedspreads of white
Gallic linen, if only it go not to
    waste that from midnight
You've sat in a place where no
    blacksmith would stay, which no man
Who teaches how to card wool with
    crooked irons would stand;
If only it go not to waste that
    you have smelled the fumes

Of as many lamps as there were boys,
    with a Horace begloomed
With stains and a Vergil black and
    sooty from sticky thumbs.

Yet rare is the fee that needs no   [228]
    order of court to see
That it's paid. But parents impose
    strict rules on teacher that he
Must break no laws of grammar, must
    read all histories, know
Every classic author as well as his
    every finger and toe;
And if caught by chance on his way
    to the baths or Phoebus' spot,
Must answer a quiz, such as Who was
    Anchises' nurse? And what
Was Anchemolus' stepmother's name?
    Where was she born? Of what line?
How long did Acestes live? And how
    many barrels of wine
From Sicily did he give the Trojans?
    Require him to form
The tender minds as if with a thumb,
    like someone who warms
And shapes a face out of wax; require
    him to be to the whole
Classroom a father, lest they play
    nasty games and take hold
Of each other. It's no easy job to
    keep the hands and the bright,
Slyly winking eyes of so many
    boys always in sight.
"Take care of all this," they say,
    "and at the end of the year
Get the gold piece the crowd demands
    for a winning charioteer."

VIII

what's the use
of a pedigree?

What's the use of a pedigree? What
    good is it being esteemed
For ancient bloodlines, Ponticus,
    flaunting statues that gleamed
In new paint once: your ancestors—
    Aemilianus, let's say,
Erect in his chariot; Curius, though
    he's half crumbled away;
Corvinus, whose shoulder is missing;
    or Galba, whose ears and nose
Are shattered? What point in boasting
    that all this splendor grows
On your rich family tree and makes
    you kin through many offshoots
To dictators and lords in the dusty
    past if your own pursuits
Under Lepidus' nose are foul? What
    do so many effigies mean,
These warriors who fought at Numantia,
    if you pursue a routine
Of shooting dice all night before
    their eyes, then fall
Into bed at dawn, just when those
    old leaders were moving all
Their standards and camps? Why should
    Fabius, born of Hercules' line,
Take pride in the name Allobrogicus
    and in his shrine,

The Great Altar, if he is greedy and
    stupid and more of a fluff
Than a Euganean lamb, if his tender
    loins, well buffed
And smooth with Catanian pumice,
    his hairy forebears disgrace?
Or if, as a buyer of poison, he defiles
    his unhappy race
With a statue that must be broken?
    Although you decorate
Your whole front hall on both sides
    with waxen masks of great
Ancestors, true nobility lies in
    virtue alone.
Have the character that in Paulus,
    Cossus, or Drusus was shown,
Rank them above your ancestral statues,
    let them precede
Your emblem itself when you are
    consul. You owe to me,
First of all, the virtues of the soul.
    Do you deserve
To be accounted blameless, stanch
    for justice, unswerved
In word and deed? I acknowledge you
    a lord. Hail to you,
Gaetulicus or Silanus, or you of
    whatever new
Bloodline, if to a rejoicing country
    you stand out
As a rare and excellent citizen, we're
    glad to shout
What Egypt shouts on finding Osiris.
    For who would call
A man noble who shames his race and
    has no distinction at all
But his famous name? We call someone's
    dwarf an "Atlas," a churl
From Africa "Snow-White," a twisted,
    hunchback girl

"Europa"; and lazy mongrels, hairless
    from chronic mange
And licking the mouths of empty oil
    flasks, men easily change
Into "Tiger," "Lion," "Panther," or
    anything else on earth
That roars more savagely. So be
    careful, and fear such mirth,
Lest you get the name of Creticus or
    Camerinus too.

[39] And whom do I lecture thus? Rubellius
    Blandus, it's you
I'm talking to. You're puffed with
    pride at your high pedigree
From the Drusi, as though you yourself
    had done something that we
Should think makes you noble; and
    at the knowledge that you got
Conceived by a girl ashine with Iulian
    blood, and not
By one who weaves for hire by the
    windswept walls. "You're dirt,"
You sneer, "the worst scum of our
    rabble, and none of you can assert
Which is the country your father was
    born in. But I am one
Of the Cecropidae." Well, viva!
    Long may you enjoy the renown
Of your origin! And yet, you'll find
    in the lowest riffraff
Some eloquent Roman who knows how
    to plead lawsuits on behalf
Of illiterate lords. The men who
    solve the riddles and split
The knots of the law come out of the
    common herd. From it
Comes forth the youthful soldier,
    earnest in duty, to march

Off to the Euphrates or to our eagle
    standards that guard
The vanquished Batavians. All the
    while you are nothing more
Than a Cecropid, exactly like a
    Hermes with four
Limbs missing. You've got only one
    advantage in this regard—
His head is of marble and yours is
    alive—but just as hard.

You descendant of Trojans, tell me,   [56]
    who considers a dumb
Tame beast well-sired unless it's
    strong? From this must come
Our praise of the fastest horse whose
    speed makes every hand burn
With applause and the Circus shout
    itself hoarse at the victory earned.
The noblest horse, in whatever pasture
    bred, is the kind
Whose dust rises first on the track,
    whose flight leaves the rest behind.
But Derby winners' offspring
    on the auction block are thrown
If Victory seldom rides their cars.
    No respect is shown
To their ancestors, their spirits
    receive no sacrifice.
These descendants are made to shift,
    and for a niggling price,
From one to another master—clodhoppers
    that only are fit
To turn mill wheels, with chafing
    necks they pull the bit
And the traces. So if I'm to honor
    you, not your goods, provide
Me with something special to you to
    inscribe with your titles besides

The honors we gave and still give
    those to whom you owe your all.

[71]   So much for the young man whom reports
    to us have recalled
As proud and puffed up with his
    kinship to Nero; for great
Concern for others is usually rare
    in such a high estate.
But Ponticus, I'd not want you
    esteemed for praise of your race
So much that you yourself do nothing
    to merit praise
In the future. It's a pitiful thing
    to rest on the fame
Of others; the pillars may go and
    the roof collapse on the frame.
A vine shoot flung to earth wants the
    elm of which it's bereft.
So be a good soldier, true to your
    wards and honest when left
To decide an issue. If called in court
    to the witness stand
For some vague and dubious suit,
    though Phalaris himself command
You to lie and bring his bull-shaped
    furnace to force you by threat
Into perjury, still believe it the
    greatest of sins to set
Your life above honor, and for the
    sake of your life to lose
The reason for living. A man who
    deserves to die, though he chews
A hundred Lucrine oysters at dinner
    and is drenched from head
To foot in whole cauldrons of Cosmus'
    perfumes, is already dead.

When at length in that long-expected   [87]
    province you accede
As governor, curb your anger, restrain
    it and your greed;
Pity our bankrupt allies, whose very
    bones are sucked dry
Of marrow. Respect what the law
    requires, respect and comply
With orders the Senate gives, consider
    the honors that lie
In store for good rulers, the lightning
    bolts the Senate can fire at
The bad ones, such as Capito and
    Numitor—each one a pirate
Of pirates of the Cilicians. And
    yet what good did it do
To condemn them? Now that Pansa has
    stripped off what few
Things Natta left you, Chaerippus,
    look for a junkman somewhere
To buy your rags. But keep it hushed
    up. With nothing to spare
But the penny for Charon's ferry,
    it's madness to lose even that.

Long ago our allies, newly conquered   [98]
    but flourishing, had
A different complaint, and the wound
    from losses was not the same.
Then all their houses were well
    supplied and they could claim
Great piles of cash and Spartan cloaks
    and purple gowns
From Cos; with Parrhasius' paintings
    and Myron's statues around,
The ivory figures of Phidias lived and
    everywhere
Many works of Polyclitus; few tables
    lacked silverware

139

By Mentor. But later there was
    Dolabella, and next
Antonius, then sacrilegious Verres
    to load the decks
Of huge freighters with smuggled
    spoils—more trophies of peace
Than of war. Today, you may grab
    from our allies if you seize
A little farm, a few yoke of oxen,
    a small drove of mares
And the stud of the herd; or the
    household gods themselves, if there's
Some notable statue, or even a single
    god, left still
In the shrine: for these, indeed,
    are your best bet, these fill
The bill nowadays as the finest things.
    You despise, perhaps,
The non-warring men of Rhodes and
    Corinth's perfumed young chaps—
And rightly: what could the depilated
    youths or the smooth
Legs of the entire nation do to you?
    But uncouth
And rugged Spain you must avoid,
    and the land of Gaul
And Dalmatia's shores. And leave
    alone those farmers who haul
Supplies to feed a city, which has
    no time for more
Than the Circus and plays: anyway,
    how great a gain would you score
From them by such dire crimes when
    Marius lately has shorn
The Africans to their skin? Above
    all, take care that no harm
Is done to men who are defeated but
    without fear.
Though you take all their gold and
    silver, you'll leave their spears

Swords, shields, and helmets;
     despoiled, they'll have weapons still.

What I've just proposed is no mere   [125]
     opinion, it's truth; you will
Believe I'm reading to you from a
     leaf the Sibyl prepared.
If your retinue is above corruption,
     if no long-haired
Favorite sells your decisions, if
     your wife's without stain
And isn't prepared, like a Harpy
     circling through all your domains
And towns with crooked claws, to
     grab all the cash in sight,
You may trace to King Picus your
     line; or if grander names delight
Your heart, you may count among your
     ancestors the whole congeries
Of the Titans and Prometheus himself,
     and after these
May choose for yourself an ancestor
     from any myth you please.
But if you're driven headlong by
     ambition and lust, if you break
Your rods on the bleeding backs of
     our allies, if you take
Delight in seeing your axes blunted
     on so many heads
That the headsman himself is worn
     out, then that nobility bred
In your own parents begins to rise
     up against you and shed
A glaring light on your shameful
     deeds. The greater the name
Of the sinner, the more conspicuous
     his sin, the greater his blame.
If you are given to signing forged
     wills, what is it to me

If you do it in temples your grandfather
      built, or if it be
At your father's triumphal statue?
      What do I care if you hide
In a hood and sneak out at night
      for adultery on the side?

[146]   Obese Lateranus flies past his
      ancestors' ashes and bones
In a speeding car and with his own
      hands this mule driver, known
To you as Consul, puts on the brakes.
      To be sure, it's night;
But the moon looks on and stars strain
      their eyes for the sight.
Lateranus will carry his whip in broad
      daylight when the end
Of his term in office comes, never
      shrink from meeting a friend,
Now old, but be the first to wave
      his whip; he'll unbind
The bales of hay and pour oats for
      his weary beasts. Meantime,
Though he slays, in Numa's fashion,
      lambs and russet steers,
He swears before Jove's high altar
      by none but his revered
Goddess of horses, and images daubed
      on the stinking stalls.
And when he wants to renew, in the
      all-night taverns, his calls,
A Syro-Phoenician, drenched in
      persistent perfume, runs out
To meet him—a Syro-Phoenician who
      lives somewhere about
The Idumean gate—and affecting the
      part of a host, he hails
Him as lord and king; and at his heels,
      Cyane trails,

With shirts tucked up and with
    a bottle of wine to sell.

An apologist for his faults will tell   [163]
    me: "We, as well,
Did all that as boys." Perhaps;
    but you stopped, of course, and fled from
Your dissolute ways. Let your days
    of wild oats be brief; let some
Of your vices be shorn with your first
    ceremonial shave. To boys
We may give a pardon; but Lateranus
    pursued the joys
Of those steaming dives with printed
    awnings when fully mature,
Fit to guard in arms Armenian and
    Syrian streams, hold secure
The Rhine and the Danube, old enough
    to act as bodyguard
To Nero. Send to Ostia, Caesar,
    send there, but charge
Your envoy to search in a big saloon;
    you'll find him there,
Stretched out right next to some
    cutthroat, mixed in somewhere
With sailors, thieves, and runaway
    slaves, among hangmen and makers
Of coffins and eunuch priests passed
    out on their now unshaken
Tambourines. Here it's free and
    equal—one cup for all,
No separate bed for anyone, and no
    table to call
Your own, apart from the others.
    What would you do if you,
Ponticus, had a slave like this?
    You'd send him right to
Your Tuscan or Lucanian penal farm,
    would you not?

But you, you scions of Troy, excuse
        yourselves; and what
Would shame a cobbler, in a Volesus
        or Brutus is grace.

[183]   What if I can never mention examples
                so shameful, so base,
        That something worse is not left out?
                When you'd gone through
        Your wealth, Damasippus, you hired
                your voice to the stage and you
        Took the role of the Noisy Ghost in
                Catullus' mime play. Then, too,
        Lightfooted Lentulus acted Laureolus
                with such conviction
        That in my view he deserved the
                bandit's real crucifixion.
        But you can't forgive the audience
                itself—the herd that sits
        Stonefaced and watches patricians
                clowning, hears the low wit
        Of a Fabius with bare feet and laughs
                at the slapstick games
        Of the noble Mamerci. Who cares how
                cheaply they sell their names?
        No Nero compels them, and yet they
                don't hesitate to sell
        Themselves for a great producer's
                shows. But suppose I tell
        You: Here are swords for death, and
                there a place on the stage.
        Which choice is more noble? Has
                any man in any age
        So feared to die that he'd be Thymele's
                cuckold in plays
        Or stooge to Corinthus, the clown?
                Yet, when an emperor's craze
        Is fiddling, it's not so strange if
                the nobles start to act.

144

Beyond this, what will be left but
    the games? And there in fact
You have the shame of our city:
    Gracchus fighting, unarmed
Even as a murmillo, without shield
    or scimitar,
For gear like this he refuses, quite
    refuses and hates,
And he doesn't hide his face in a
    helmet. Look what he shakes—
A trident! And after he has cast
    with a shaky right hand
His trailing net to no purpose, he
    raises to the grandstand
His bare face for all to recognize
    and runs all around
The arena. We know that tunic, with
    gold trim stretching down
From his throat and braid hung from
    the cap with a lofty crown.
And so the fighter ordered to battle
    Gracchus endured
More grievous shame than any wound
    would have procured.

If free suffrage were given the people,   [211]
    who'd be so mad as not
To choose Seneca over Nero, for whose
    punishment there ought
To have been prepared not just one
    sack with one ape and one
Adder? His crime was like that of
    Agamemnon's son,
But the motive makes it a different
    matter: indeed, ordained
By the gods' command, Orestes avenged
    his father, slain
In his cups. He never slit Electra's
    throat, nor stained

145

Himself with the blood of his Spartan
    wife, nor mixed aconite
For his kin; he never sang on the
    stage, nor did he write
An epic of Troy! For which of Nero's
    acts in his fierce
And bloody tyranny was more deserving
    to be avenged
By the arms of Verginius, Vindex, or
    Galba? These were the arts,
The works of our noble prince: prostituting
    himself to play parts
On a foreign stage with godawful
    singing, but loving it
And winning a Greek parsley crown!
    Let your forbears' statues sit
With the trophies won by your voice,
    and lay at Domitius' feet
The long robe of Antigone or Thyestes,
    the mask and attire
Of Melanippa, and hang on a marble
    colossus your lyre!

[231]   Where can nobler ancestors be found
    than yours, Catiline,
Or yours, Cethegus? Yet you plotted
    night raids, with design
To burn our homes and temples, as
    though you were sons of Gauls
In trousers or of the Senones, daring
    deeds that call
For pitch-lined torture shirts. But
    our consul on watch has stood
And repelled your troops. Born in
    Arpinum, of common blood,
A knight from the provinces, new to
    Rome, he posts armed guards
Everywhere to protect the frightened
    people and labors hard

On every hill. Thus within the
    walls his toga obtained
For him renown and honor as great
    as Octavius gained
By the battle at Actium or by his
    sword, dripping steadily
From constant slaughter out on the
    plains of Thessaly.
But Rome was still free when she
    hailed Cicero as parent and sire
Of his country! Another man from
    Arpinum used to hire
Himself as a tenant farmer on Volscian
    hill-farms and tire
His limbs at another's plow; after
    that, enlisted, he'd know
The crack of a knotty club on his
    head if his spade was slow
And lazy in piling walls for the camp.
    Yet this man braves
The Teutonic invaders and utmost perils,
    alone he saves
The terrified city. And so, after
    vultures, who never had met
Bigger corpses, flew down on the
    slaughtered Cimbri, the nobly bred
Colleague of Marius was adorned with
    the second bay.

Plebeian the souls of the Decii,   [254]
    plebeian their names, but they
Were good enough for the gods of the
    underworld and, too,
For Mother Earth in lieu of all the
    legions, in lieu
Of all the allies and youth of
    Latium, for the two
Decii were more worthwhile than those
    who were saved by them.

[259] Born of a slave girl was he who won
        the robe, diadem,
      And emblems of Quirinus—the last of
        our good kings.
      The sons of the consul himself, however,
        were ready to spring
      The locks on the city gates in treason,
        admitting the tyrants
      From their exile, when they would
        better have been aspirants
      To some great deed for threatened
        freedom—some act to command
      Admiration from Mucius or Horatius
        or the girl who swam
      Across the Tiber, the boundary of
        our domain. A slave,
      Who should be mourned by our matrons,
        was the one who gave
      Their secret plot to the Senate.
        But they got their just deserts
      From scourges and the ax, then under
        the law used first.

[269] I'd rather Thersites were your father,
        if only you
      Were like Aeacus' grandson, able to
        take unto
      Yourself the armor of Vulcan, than
        that Achilles begot
      You, and you be like Thersites.
        And yet, no matter to what
      Far time you trace your name, no
        matter how long your race,
      In the end you derive your family
        from an infamous place

Of refuge: Your first ancestor,
    whatever you may claim,
Was either a shepherd or else—something
    I'd rather not name.

the woes of
a male hustler

I'd like to know why so often,
    Naevolus, when we meet
You're gloomy, with face screwed up
    like Marsyas in defeat.
Why should you look like Ravola,
    caught at his diving trick,
With beard sopping wet, in Rhodope's
    cranny? If slaves take a lick
At sweetmeats, we give them a whipping.
    You look more desolate
Than Crepereius Pollio, who offers
    three times the rate
Of interest all over town and can't
    find a sucker. Why so
Many wrinkles suddenly? You used to
    be well contented, I know,
A society playboy of sorts, with
    caustic jibes and a flow
Of cocktail-party jokes. Now it's
    changed; you look down in
The mouth, your hair an unkempt,
    unpomaded thatch, your skin
With no sheen such as hot packs
    of birdlime gave it, your limbs
Untidy and grizzled with sprouting
    hair. What makes you as grim

And thin as a constantly sick old roué
    in whom there burns
A quartan fever long since completely
    at home? One discerns
In an ailing body the hidden torments,
    as well as delights,
Of the soul: the face shows the mood
    of either. You seem to have quite
Changed your way of life, therefore—
    to be doing a turnabout
On your past. A short while back,
    I recall, you used to hang out
At the temple of Isis, the Ganymede
    in the shrine of Peace,
And the secret courts of that
    Imported Mother and of Ceres—
For in what temple do women not sell
    themselves? To all these
You were a more scandalous lecher
    than Aufidius, and what
You fail to tell, you'd as soon take
    on their husbands as not.

"By this kind of life many men are   [27]
    rich, but I haven't made
Very much from it to show for my
    labors. Sometimes I'm paid
With a greasy cloak to protect my
    toga, dyed a dull
And ugly color and crudely woven from
    uncombed wool
In Gaul, or a silver trinket—not
    sterling. But destiny rules
All mankind, even those parts we hide.
    For the greatest of tools,
Of inconceivable size, won't help if
    your stars are averse,
Though Virro with drooling lips looks
    on you naked and stirs

You with many tempting letters constantly.
    What can you do?
As the Greeks have put it: Men are
    attracted to queers. But who
In the world is a more insufferable
    ass than a stingy fairy?
'I paid you well,' he says, 'not once
    but twice. And not very
Long since, you got much more.' He
    adds in his head and enjoys
His fondling of me. Let's check the
    records, call in the boys
Who keep your expense accounts. It
    comes to two hundred all told.
Then count the service I've given:
    You think it's easy to hold
An erection and push it in till it
    meets your last night's meal?
The poor slave who plows your fields
    is better off in this deal
Than I who plow his master. Indeed,
    you used to think
You were thin, boyish, handsome,
    and worthy to bear Jove's drink.
But will you creatures, unwilling to
    pay for your foul escapades,
Ever show gratitude to poor old
    chums or pieces of trade?
Just look at you! What a beauty,
    to hope for presents at all!
Yet on birthdays I send big amber
    balls or a green parasol;
Or when rainy spring begins and on
    a chaise longue you loll
To handle your secret presents,
    something for Mother's Day.

[54]   "Now tell me, old goat, for whom do
    you keep so great an array

Of hills and Apulian farms—all those
    pastures that weary the hawks?
Your Campanian vineyards load you with
    rich produce from their stalks,
And slopes overlooking Cumae and
    empty Gaurus do likewise—
For who has more sealed barrels of
    wine more sure of time
To mature? How much would you notice
    the loss if you gave a few
Of those acres to a client whose
    loins were exhausted on you?
Now wouldn't it make more sense if
    you willed that country lad,
His mother, the house, his
    playmate pup, to me instead
Of to some friend who beats the cymbals?
    'You're in bad taste
When you beg,' he says. But my rent
    cries out to me, Beg! And I'm faced
With pleas of my lone slave boy—lone
    as Polyphemus' great eye,
Which helped the crafty Ulysses
    escape. I'll have to buy
A second boy, for this one's not
    enough, and feed
Them both. What am I to do when
    winter blows? What, indeed,
Shall I say to the shoulders and feet
    of my slaves when the north wind numbs
In December? 'Stiff upper lip—wait
    till the grasshoppers come'?

"And though you ignore or slight my   [70]
    other services, what
Fair price would you put on this one
    favor—that if I were not
Your devoted, loyal client, your wife
    would be virgin right now?

You know how often you asked me, and
    by what means, and your vow
To reward me well. Many times I've
    caught the girl and twined
Her in my embrace as she fled your
    home with divorce in mind,
A genuine husband in view. Working
    hard all night in your stead,
I scarcely paid your debt, while you
    sniffled outside. The bed
Is my witness, and you yourself who
    could hear the squeak of springs
And your wife's own voice. Many a
    shaky marriage, where things
Were falling apart, the union all
    but dissolved, has been
By some adulterer saved. Can you
    think of an out? Which, then,
Of my services do you account the
    greatest, which the least?
Do I get no credit, treacherous
    ingrate, for having increased
Your family, siring a little son or
    daughter for you?
For you are bringing them up, and
    you love to put on view
In the records proof of your
    manhood. Hang garlands on your doors—
You're now a father! I've given you
    something you can oppose
To gossip. You have the rights of
    a parent; thanks to me,
You're written down as the heir, you
    receive the whole legacy,
Not to mention a nice windfall to
    boot. Besides, there'll be
Many more advantages added to such a
    bequest if I raise
The count of your children to the
    full three."

                    You have a just case,   [90]
        Naevolus, for your complaint. But
            what does he say in defense?

        "He shrugs it off and looks for   [92]
            another two-legged, dense
        Jackass like me. But remember to hide
            what I have confessed
        To you alone, and keep my complaints
            hushed up in your breast.
        For it's courting death to have a foe
            who smoothes his skin
        With pumice. The man who not long
            ago had let me in
        On a secret now burns with rage and
            hates me, as if I've betrayed
        Whatever I know. He won't hesitate
            to use a blade,
        To split my head with a club, or set
            fire to my house. Nor can
        You ignore or dismiss the fact that
            for so wealthy a man
        The cost of poison is never high.
            So keep well hid
        My secrets, as well as the Council
            of Mars in Athens did."

[102]   O Corydon, Corydon! Do you suppose
            that a rich man keeps
        Any secrets? Though his slaves may
            hold their tongues, his beasts
        Of burden, his dog, the gateposts,
            and marble columns will talk.
        He may shut the windows, cover
            cracks with curtains, lock

The doors, douse the light, make
    everyone leave, let no one sleep
Near at hand: but before the dawn the
    neighborhood barkeep
Will know what he was doing at second
    cock crow, will hear
Also what his chief cooks and carvers
    invented. For what smear,
What crime do they hesitate to lay
    on their masters so long
As their floggings are avenged by
    slander? Nor will you be wrong
In thinking some tippler looks for
    you in the streets to pour
In your wretched ear, willynilly, his
    drunken tale. Therefore,
Ask them what you begged of me just
    now, let *them* hush up.
Why, they'd rather blurt out a secret
    than drink as many cups
Of stolen wine as Saufeia, when making
    a sacrifice
For the people, used to guzzle.
    One should lead a clean life,
For many reasons, but chiefly for this
    one: You may despise
The gossip of slaves. For a tongue's
    the worst part of bad slaves.
And yet worse still is the man who
    won't get rid of the knaves
Whose rumors and bellies feed on his
    money and food supplies.

[124] "A fine sermon you've given, but a
    cliché. What do you advise
Me now to do, with time wasted,
    hopes crushed? For like a flower
The brief span of our poor unhappy
    life to its final hour

Is hastening on; and while we drink
    and call for gay wreaths,
Perfumes, and young girls, old age
    creeps upon us, unperceived."

Oh, don't be afraid. So long as our   [130]
    Seven Hills stand there,
You'll never lack queer friends.
    They flock in from everywhere
In wagons and on ships—all that
    breed who scratch their heads
With just one finger. Another better
    prospect is spread
Before you now—only take your doses
    of Spanish fly.

"Fine talk for fortunate men! But   [135]
    my Fates rejoice if I
By my prick's hard labor can fill my
    belly. Lares, O my
Little household gods, whom I entreat
    always with some grains
Of incense or meal or a tiny garland,
    when shall I obtain
Anything like enough to keep me safe,
    when I am old,
From a beggar's stick and rags? A
    few thousand at interest controlled
By sound investment is all I need—
    and some dishes of good
Plain silver, but not so plain the
    censor Fabricius would
Not have condemned them, and two
    sturdy men from Serbian tribes
To carry my chair on their shoulders
    so I at ease may ride
To my place in the roaring circus.
    And let me have, besides,

A stooped engraver, and someone else
    who'll paint with a sure,
Quick brush many portraits of me.
    That's enough, since I'll be poor.
Such pitiful prayers, not even a hope
    for them, I fear.
For when I pray to Fortune for help,
    she plugs up her ears
With beeswax fetched from the same
    ship that brought Ulysses through
The Sicilian sirens' trap when that
    wax had deafened his crew."

X

the vanity of human wishes

In all the lands that spread from
    Cadiz to the Ganges and on
To the East, few can distinguish
    true blessings from ills, free from
The cloud of error. For what do we
    covet or fear by force
Of reason? What plan do you set on
    such a propitious course
That you don't repent of your effort
    and your answered prayer?
The softhearted gods have wrecked
    whole families, granting their
Own wishes. In martial gear or togas
    we pray for what
Will bring our ruin upon us. And
    many a man has begot
His death by the babbling flood of his
    eloquence, and one
By trusting strength and musclebound
    arms; but more have been done
To death by money they cared too
    much to accumulate
And by incomes that exceeded all
    paternal estates
As much as the British whale exceeds
    the dolphin's weight.

That's why Longinus and super-rich
    Seneca's huge private park
Were blockaded by soldiers on Nero's
    orders in those dark
And terrible times, and the excellent
    Lateran palace thrown
Under siege by a full battalion:
    soldiers rarely go
Into garrets. Although but few plain
    silver bowls you take
On a trip by night, you'll fear for
    clubs and knives and quake
At the shadow of a reed that in the
    moonlight sways.
A man who has nothing can whistle
    in a robber's face.

[23]   Almost the first prayer, best known
    in every temple, calls
For wealth, that riches increase,
    that our coffer be biggest in all
The forum. But no aconite is drunk
    from earthenware cups;
Beware the time when you lift a
    jeweled goblet up
And Setine wine sparkles red in the
    golden bowl. Therefore,
Will you not praise those two wise
    men, one of whom used to roar
With laughter, the other burst into
    tears, every time they set
One foot beyond the door and stepped
    outside? And yet
The censure of hooting laughter is
    easy for anyone;
What's wondrous is where the other
    found enough water to run
From his eyes. Democritus' sides
    with constant laughter ached,

Though in his cities there were no
    robes such as we make,
Purple-edged and striped, no fasces,
    no tribunals or litters.
Suppose he'd seen a praetor, perched
    in a chariot's glitter
Above dust clouds of the circus, the
    palm-embroidered cloak
Of Jupiter on his shoulders and
    trailing—about to choke
At its weight—a gold-braided Tyrian
    cloak hung at his throat,
Flaunting a crown so huge no head
    could support it? But note
The sweating slave who must hold the
    crown and also ride
In the chariot with his master to
    temper the consul's pride!
Then, add the bird spreading wings
    from his ivory scepter, a band
Of trumpeters flanking files of
    clients who show on command,
And white-robed citizens, marching
    in front with reins in hand—
Friends won by a tiny dole stuck in
    their purses. Even then
The sage found topics for laughter
    each time he met fellowmen:
His wisdom shows that distinguished
    men, who will set us clear
And great examples, may still be born
    in the dense atmosphere
Of Numbskull Land. He laughed at
    the troubles and indeed
The joys of the common folk, sometimes
    at their tears, while he'd
Himself tell Fortune, if she were
    threatening him, just to
Go hang, and poke his middle finger
    out—*Screw you!*

[54] Thus what we pray for, things for
    which it's proper and right
To load the knees of the gods with
    wax, are either quite
Unprofitable or pernicious. Great
    power, which incites
Great envy, hurls some men to
    destruction; they are drowned
In a long, splendid stream of honors.
    Their statues fall to the ground,
Pulled down by ropes, then axblows
    break even chariot wheels
And the legs of innocent horses.
    And now the blazes leap
And roar, with bellows in the forges;
    the head, by the crowd
Adored, is burning, and mighty
    Sejanus cracks; then out
Of that face, once next to chief of
    all the world, are shaped
Pitchers, skillets, basins, and chamber
    pots. Then drape
Bay leaves on your door! Lead a big
    chalky bull to the Capitol
To offer. Sejanus is dragged by a
    hook to be seen by all,
And all rejoice. "What lip, what a
    look on his face, he had!
Believe me, truly I never liked that
    man. But how bad
Was the charge that finished him?
    Who informed? What evidence,
What witness, proved the case?"
    "It wasn't like that. An immense
Long-winded letter was sent from
    Capri." "All right, I've got
Your meaning. That's all I need
    to know."

                    But tell me, what   [72]
Of Remus' spawn? As always, it
    follows fortune and hates
Condemned men. This same mob—if
    Nortia, goddess of fate,
Had favored her Tuscan, if the emperor
    had been struck down
In safe old age—would have named
    Sejanus in that same hour
Augustus. The public, now for a
    long time, ever since there
Was no one to whom to sell our votes,
    has flung off its cares;
For the people, who once bestowed
    authority, army commands,
Consulships, and everything else,
    today keep their hands
To themselves and for just two things
    do they eagerly yearn:
Bread and the games.

                    "I hear that many   [81]
    are scheduled to burn."
"No doubt about it. A big hot
    furnace is going." "My friend
Bruttidius, when we met at the altar
    of Mars, looked then
Rather pale. What I fear is that
    our Ajax, in defeat,
Will exact revenge for poor defense."
    "Let's run full speed
To the river and kick our Caesar's
    enemy while he lies
On the bank." "But let our slaves
    see, so that none testifies
Against us and drags his master,
    trembling, into a court

With a halter round his neck."

[88]   This was
    the talk they report
As common back then on Sejanus—this
    the underground voice
Of the mob. Wouldn't you have
    loved to be Sejanus, rejoice
In his popularity, have as much wealth,
    bestow every prize
Of high office, name generals of
    armies, be in all eyes
The proxy of that emperor, perched
    on a ledge in steep
Capri, with flocks of Chaldean
    soothsayers around like sheep?
Of course you'd like the soldiers,
    cavalry squadrons, the fine
Private guard in your barracks!
    Why shouldn't you? Even those who decline
To kill would like the power to kill.
    But what bright fame
Or great fortune is worth it if your
    enjoyment incurs the same
Degree of sorrows to come? Would
    you rather wear the rich gown
Of this man who's dragged in the
    streets or be mayor of some small town
Like Podunk, or maybe a ragged
    inspector in dull Endsville,
Checking weights and measures,
    smashing a quart pot or a gill
If it's short? Then Sejanus didn't
    know, you'll admit, what ought
To be wished. For he who craved too
    many honors and sought
Too much wealth was building, story
    by story, the lofty tower

From which his fall would be greater,
    his headlong crash from power
To ruin the more enormous. What was
    it that overthrew
The Crassi and the Pompeii, and
    him, that Caesar who drew
The subdued Romans under his scourge?
    What else but desire
For highest rank, pursued by fair
    means or foul, and the ire
Of the spiteful gods who made ambitious
    prayers come true?
Few kings descend to Ceres' son-in-law
    except through
Deep wounds or murder, few tyrants
    through a bloodless death.

The schoolboy prays through his   [114]
    holidays in each second breath
For Demosthenes' or Cicero's eloquence
    and renown,
When he's had his first dollar's
    worth of wisdom, escorted through town
By a slave to guard his thin book
    satchel. Yet this very
Eloquence brought both orators death.
    The extraordinary,
Full, overflowing springs of genius
    in each one led
To death. His own genius cut off
    Cicero's hands and head;
Never yet has a petty lawyer's blood
    on the rostra been shed.
"O fortunate, when made consul was
    I, was Rome," he wrote.
If Cicero always had spoken thus, he
    might have shown
Contempt for Antony's swords. I'll
    settle for verse designed

To be laughed at, rather than you,
    O notably famous, divine
Philippic that rolls out after the
    first! And terrible, too,
Was the death that snatched off
    Demosthenes, an orator who
Thrilled Athens with sweeping speech
    and held in rein the filled
Theater. Under an evil star and
    under ill will
Of the gods this man was born, he
    whom his father, blear-eyed
With soot from glowing ore, sent
    away from the forge's side,
From the coals, the tongs, the anvil
    that to swords imparts
A temper, from grimy Vulcan, to
    study rhetorical art.

[133] The spoils of war, displayed on the
    trophy tree—breast plate,
Broken helmet, dangling visor,
    chariot yoke snapped straight
From the shaft, the ensign of
    captured warships—and a woebegone
Prisoner perched on an arch of triumph,
    they look upon
As glories greater than human good.
    For these the Greek,
The Roman, and all the outlandish
    generals always seek;
For these they endure great toil
    and danger—the thirst for fame
Is so much greater than for virtue!
    For who would embrace
Virtue herself if you stripped away
    her rewards? And yet
In the past a country has often with
    its destruction met

By the vainglory of a few, by their
    lust for praise, to own
A title to cling to the stones that
    guard their ashes—stones
That the ruinous strength of a
    barren fig tree can undermine
And split, since even to sepulchers
    doom is also assigned.

Put Hannibal on the scales. What   [147]
    will you find he weighs—
That supreme commander? This is the
    man who felt Africa's space
Too cramped, though spread from
    crashing Moorish seas to sands
Of the tepid Nile, from Ethiop tribes
    to new elephant lands!
He adds to his empire Spain, he
    vaults the Pyrenees;
Then Nature blocks his march with
    Alps and snow: but these
He conquers, shatters boulders
    with vinegar, blasts cliffsides,
And there lies Italy in his hand!
    Still onward he rides,
Crying, "Nothing's finished till
    Punic soldiers break apart
The gates of Rome and I plant my flag
    in the city's heart!"
Oh, what a sight it was, how worthy,
    significant,
For a painting—this one-eyed general
    riding an elephant!
So how did he end? Oh, dreams of
    glory! Defeated, he fled
As fast as he could into exile, and
    sat, a discredited
But impressive and mighty suppliant
    in a king's anteroom

Till it pleased his Bithynian highness
    to rise. The final doom
Of him who once threw the world
    into havoc came not by sword
Nor spear nor stone, but by what
    would avenge Cannae's horde
Of dead in their oceans of blood—a
    poisoned ring. So run,
You madman, run over wild,
    frozen Alps to become just one
Of those delights of schoolboys, a
    subject for declamations!

[168]   One world was not enough for young
    Alexander—his patience
Wore thin; he fretted at earth's
    narrow limits, as though confined
On Gyara's rocks or Seriphos; yet
    after he'd gone inside
The city walled by brick makers,
    the width of a grave was enough.
Only death reveals what a nothing
    the body of man is. Such stuff
As ships once sailing through Mount
    Athos, and all the tales
Greek histories lie about—how those
    same ships under sail
Paved the sea and made a solid road
    for chariot wheels;
How deep rivers shrank and brooks
    were drunk dry at the Persians' meals;
To say nothing of all those flights
    of song, on wine-sodden wing,
That Sostratus warbled—we've heard
    it all! But how did that king
Return from Salamis—that barbarian,
    wont in his rage
To flog Corus and Eurus (who never
    inside the prison cage

Of Aeolus suffered such a thing), he
    who had chained
Earthshaking Poseidon himself, in
    this, indeed, quite restrained
For thinking him not worth branding
    too: What god would serve
Such a man? How did he return? In
    a single ship, of course,
On blood-red waves, his slow prow
    nudging through a thick tide
Of corpses. This price he paid for
    glory so long desired!

"Give me long life, O Jupiter, life   [188]
    to last many years!"
You pray for only this, whether
    sick or well. Yet how fierce,
How unceasing the miseries that
    protracted old age sustains!
First of all, the face, distorted,
    hideous, not the same
As it used to be—rough hide instead
    of skin, and cheeks
Sagging in wattles, wrinkles as
    carved as those that streak
A she-baboon's face where the shady
    glades of Thabraca stand.
In many ways young men differ—this
    one is handsomer than
That one, and he than another; one's
    muscular, one slim.
Old men look alike, with voices
    shaking like their limbs,
Heads now gone bald, childhood's
    runny noses, toothless gums
With which their bread has to be
    munched, poor things. They become
So revolting to themselves, wives,
    children, and family

That even Cossus, a legacy hunter,
    in loathing would flee.
Not the same, with palate grown dull,
    the joys of wine and food;
And as for fucking, it's long forgotten,
    or if you should
Undertake to do it, your penis lies
    there shriveled, and though
You jerk all night, it still
    lies limp. Is this hoary old
Feeble member something to wish for?
    Why shouldn't lust be suspect,
With good cause, that pretends to
    fornication with nothing erect?

[209] Now observe the loss of another sense:
    What joy can he know
In a singer, be he the best, or
    Seleucus' harping or those
Whose custom it is to shine in
    gold-embroidered robes?
What does it matter where in the
    huge theater his chair
May be when he is scarcely able
    to hear the blare
Of horns or trumpets in chorus?
    The slave, to make him hear
The name of a guest or the time of
    day, must shout in his ear.

[217] Besides, the thin blood left in his
    chilly body grows warm
With nothing but fever. All sorts
    of diseases, in the form
Of troops on the march, parade around
    him. Ask me their names
And I could reveal more quickly the
    lovers Oppia claimed,

The patients Themison killed in one
    autumn, the partners done in
By Basilus, the orphans defrauded
    by Hirrus; or how many men
Long-legged Maura wears out in one
    day, how many boys
The teacher Hamillus defiles. I
    could sooner run through an invoice
Of villas now owned by the barber
    whose razor used to scrape
My tough beard when I was young.
    One man has pains in his nape,
One in the loins, a third in the hips;
    one's lost both eyes
And envies the one-eyed man; another
    with pale lips tries
To eat from a nurse's fingers; and
    this one who used to spread
His jaws wide open at the mere sight
    of dinner instead
Now gapes like a baby swallow whose
    fasting mother flies back
With a beak full of food. But worse
    than any physical lack
Is a failing mind, which forgets
    the names of slaves, the face
Of a friend with whom he dined
    last night, or those of his race,
The children he has fathered and
    reared. For by his scrawl
On a cruel will he strips his own
    heirs, and Phiale gets all
His estate—so great is the power
    of her expert lips,
Which had worked for many years with
    a brothel membership.

Though mental powers be strong, he   [240]
    still must bear his sons

171

To their funerals and must look on
       pyres of beloved ones—
His wife, his brothers—and urns
       filled with his sisters' ashes.
This is the punishment of those who
       live long: death slashes
One after another in their homes,
       and woes untold
Abound, and they, in constant grief
       and black weeds, grow old.
The king of Pylos, if in great Homer
       you put any trust,
Was an instance of life almost as
       long as the crow. He must
Have been happy, of course, that he
       had put off death for so
Many generations, now counting on
       his fingers his score
Of years, and had drunk new wine so
       often. I beg you, please,
For a moment, note how he complains
       of the Fates' decrees
And his too-long thread of life when
       in the flames he sees
His brave Antilochus' beard and
       asks of all his friends
Why he has lived to this day and in
       what deed he has sinned
To deserve such long old age. Of
       the same thing Peleus complains
When he mourns his lost Achilles;
       also that other whose fate
It was to grieve sea-roving Ulysses.
       With Troy unscathed,
King Priam might have gone down to
       Assaracus' shade
In royal, solemn pomp while Hector
       and all his brothers
Bore the corpse on their shoulders
       through weeping Trojan mothers,

And Cassandra gave her first wail
    of woe and Polyxena tore
Her clothes, if he only had died at
    a different time, before
His Paris had started to construct
    audacious ships.
What joy, then, did long life bring
    him? He saw the eclipse
Of his world, all in ruins, Asia
    dying by fire and the sword.
Then laying aside his crown, he
    armed himself, an age-scored,
Quavering soldier, and fell before
    great Jupiter's shrine
Like an old ox, now despised by the
    thankless plow, who inclines
A poor, thin neck to his conqueror's
    knife. At least he died
The death of a human being. But
    that to his wife was denied,
Who lived after him to bark with a
    savage dog's open mouth.

I hasten to treat of our own   [273]
    countrymen and so leave out
Mithridates, king of Pontus, and
    Croesus, warned in advance
By wise Solon's eloquent words to
    think on the last expanse
Of a long lifetime. To Marius this
    brought prison and led
To the swamps of Minturnae, to exile,
    to begging his bread
In conquered Carthage. What could
    Nature, what could Rome,
Have ever produced in the world more
    blest with glory than
That citizen if he had breathed his
    great soul out as he,

After marching captive troops in the
    full pomp of victory,
Was about to step from his German
    chariot? That kindly land
Campania gave Pompey a fever he
    should have wanted; but bands
Of cities, with public prayers, won
    out. So his own good luck
And Rome's saved him to face defeat
    and get his head struck
From his body. Lentulus missed
    this disgrace; Cethegus died
With body intact; no insult on
    Catiline's corpse was tried.

[289] On seeing the temple of Venus, an
    anxious mother will pray
In a whisper, O may her sons be
    handsome; then louder, O may
Her daughters be lovely beyond her
    fondest dreams. "But why
Should I be blamed?" she asks;
    "Latona's delighted by
Her fair Diana." But Lucretia forbids
    us to pray for a face
As lovely as her own; Verginia would
    gladly place
Rutilia's hump on herself and give
    Rutilia her grace.
Moreover, a son with handsome features
    always gives
His parents distress and fear—so
    rarely does beauty live
At peace with chastity. Though his
    austere home handed down
To him pure morals, like those in
    the ancient Sabines found,
And generous Nature, besides, with
    bountiful hand bestowed

A pure disposition and cheeks that
    with blushes modestly glow
(What better can Nature, more potent
    and careful than any guard,
Confer on a youth?), even so, he
    still will find it hard
To be a man. For the prodigal vice
    of a pervert will dare
To tempt even parents themselves.
    Trust money to soothe any care!
No tyrant has ever castrated ugly boys
    behind doors
Of his terrible castle; Nero ravished
    no youth with sores
Or a clubfoot, nor one with a potbelly
    or a hump on his back.

Go on, enjoy your son's good looks;   [310]
    he'll find no lack
Of great dangers ahead. He'll become
    a well-known male whore
And fear whatever revenge angry
    cuckolds may have in store;
He'll have no better luck than Mars,
    and surely he'll fall
In the net. But sometimes anguish
    exacts more than any law
Allows: by the sword one adulterer
    dies, from cutting hides
Another bleeds, and some get a mullet
    shoved inside.
But your sweet Endymion will be the
    stud of just that single
Matron he loves? Not for long:
    Servilia next gives a jingle
Of coins and he's hers; and he, who
    loves her not, will strip
Every jewel from her. For what can
    any female, ladyship

On down to trollop, deny to those
     wet organs? Therein
Lie all the morals of an inferior
     woman. "But then,
How does beauty hurt the chaste?"
     Well, how did a solemn oath
Help Hippolytus or Bellerophon?
     As though she were loathed
And rejected, Phaedra of course flared
     up; and in her own way,
No less than the Cretan, Stheneboea
     burned; and they
Both whipped themselves into fury.
     For woman is never so fierce
As when her hatred is goaded by shame.

[329]   Well then,
     what appears
To you to be sound advice for the lad
     that Caesar's wife
Has decided to marry? The wretched
     youth can see his life
Is being dragged to its doom by Queen
     Messalina's eyes,
For he's the handsomest of a patrician
     house—the prize.
She sits a long time, with bridal veil
     ready; the nuptial bed
Of Tyrian stuffs is publicly spread
     in the gardens; he'll get
A dowry of thousands—an ancient
     rite to which she clings:
Soothsayer and witnesses will be
     there. You thought these things
Were secret and known to only a few?
     But she will not,
Except in a legal process, marry.
     So tell me, what

Do you choose? Say no, you'll have
    to die before lamps are lit;
Commit the bigamous crime, you'll have
    a reprieve for a bit,
Till the tale, already spread through
    the city, reaches the ear
Of the Emperor Claudius. He'll be
    the last of all to hear
Of dishonor to his own house.
    Meanwhile, if a few more days
Of life are worth it, obey her commands.
    Whatever way
You may decide is the easier one or
    the better course,
You'll have to give that fair white
    neck of yours to the sword.

Then men should pray for nothing?   [346]
    If you want my advice,
You'll let the gods themselves bestow
    what may suffice
For your good and be most useful to
    your affairs. For in place
Of what we enjoy, they'll give what
    best befits our case:
Man is more precious to them than to
    himself. We're spurred
By a wish in our hearts, by urgent,
    blind desire we're stirred—
We pray for a wife and issue. But
    only the gods can foresee
What kind of wife and children we'll
    get. Still, so there'll be
Something left to pray for, some
    reason to offer at a shrine
Those entrails and white pig sausages
    that are called divine,
You should pray for this: A sound
    mind in a sound body. Pray

For courageous spirit that's not
    afraid of death and can say
Long life is the least of nature's
    gifts; that can endure
Any troubles, harbors no wrath,
    covets nothing, and feels sure
That Hercules' toils and grueling
    labors are better to bear
Than Sardanapalus' orgies and banquets
    and cushioned chair.
I'm pointing out simply what you
    can give yourself. For the one
True path to peaceful life must
    surely through virtue run.
O Fortune, you'd have no divine
    attributes if we were wise:
It's we who make you a goddess and
    set you high in the skies!

XI

a simple dinner at home

If Atticus dines on sumptuous meals,
    he's thought refined;
If Rutilus does it, he's crazy. For
    what's the public inclined
To greet with louder horselaughs
    than some Apicius, flat broke?
Every theater, tavern, bath, dinner
    party must hear its joke
About Rutilus. For, though young,
    with stalwart form, truly bred
For an army helmet, though hot-blooded
    still, he rushes ahead
In luxury so that he'll have to
    sign—not forced to this plight,
Not forbidden by any officials,
    either—and learn how to fight
Under royal decrees and mandates in
    some gladiatorial school.
You see lots of his type, awaited
    by much-put-off creditors who'll
Be lurking at the fish-market gate
    to catch them. Such men
Have only one aim in life—their
    palates. The worse pinch he's in,
The more lavish, delicious, his dinner.
    These wrecks, beginning to crack
Like ruins already, must quickly topple.
    Meanwhile they ransack

179

Every element, seeking new delicacies—
    and a wildly high price
Never hinders them in their wishes.
    And if you look at it twice,
The more it costs, the more it's
    enjoyed. Oh well, it's not hard
To raise cash to squander thus if
    they're willing to pawn a scarred,
Cracked bust of Mom, and the silver
    plate. With what they get,
They dine on luscious dainties, but
    served on an earthenware set,
Before they're reduced at last to
    gladiators' hash.
The point is, who gives the banquet?
    If Rutilus, then it's rash
Extravagance; but if Ventidius, then
    it's a laudable night—
He's got the means to afford such
    fame!

[23]   I'm sure I'm right
In despising a man who knows how much
    higher Mount Atlas rises
Than all the hills in Libya and yet,
    in comparing the sizes
Of wallets to money chests, can't see
    they're different.
Know Thyself is a heaven-sent maxim,
    which all on the heart should imprint
And keep well in mind, whether you
    seek a wife or a seat
In the sacred Senate. Not even
    Thersites asked to compete
For Achilles' armor, in which Ulysses
    made such a fool
Of himself. If you're planning to
    defend an important suit

Of doubtful merits, take a look at
    yourself and avow
What you are—a convincing lawyer or
    just a big loudmouth
Like Curtius or Matho? A man must
    know his true limitation
And observe it in big and little
    affairs, even in relation
To buying fish, so he won't drool
    for mullet when his purse
Can only afford sardines. For what
    end will you meet, with a curse
Of shrinking funds and a swelling
    gullet upon you, when all
Your inherited money and goods are
    sunk in a gut that can hold
Your capital, solid silver, cattle,
    and real estate?
The last thing, after all else,
    from which such men separate
Is the ring; and Pollio begs with
    fingers bare. What they've
To fear, the luxury lovers, is not
    the untimely grave
Nor the bitter pyre but, more fearful
    to them than death, old age.

The usual pattern is this: borrow   [46]
    money in Rome, engage
In squandering it before the lender's
    eyes, and then,
While a little—who knows how much?—
    is left and the lender begins
To grow pale, skip out and run to
    Baiae for the oyster season.
For today it's thought no worse to
    leave Rome for this reason
Than move from stifling midtown
    rooms to the Esquiline Hill.

But one affliction, one sacrifice,
    makes the exiles ill—
For one whole season they'll have to
    miss the circus games!
Not a drop of blood is left in their
    cheeks for blushes; Shame
Flees the city in ridicule and few
    would ask her to stay.

[56]   Today, dear Persicus, you will learn
    whether I obey
The excellent maxims that I preach,
    both in my deeds
And in my ways of living; or if
    while praising beans
I'm a secret gourmand and loudly
    order my slave: "Prepare
My hominy grits," but whisper "Soufflé"
    in his ear. You'll swear
That I'm an Evander, now that you've
    promised to be my guest,
And you're Hercules—or Aeneas, not
    so great or so blest,
Though both had the blood of gods
    and were carried, one by fire,
One by water, to heaven. Well, here's
    the menu, with nothing acquired
In any marketplace: From my Tivoli farm
    you'll get
A fat kid, the tenderest of the flock,
    that doesn't know yet
What grass is, never has dared to
    nibble harsh willow twigs,
And contains more milk than blood;
    asparagus my foreman's wife digs
In the mountains after work at the
    loom; big eggs warm within
The twisted straw, feathers
    sticking, and with them the hens

That laid them. Next will be grapes,
    in storage for months but still
As plump as though on the vines, two
    kinds of pears, and to fill
The baskets, apples that smell newly
    ripe and rival those
Of Picenum. You needn't fear them
    now that winter's cold
Has removed their autumn dryness and
    dangers of green juice.

Such was the meal our Senate, already   [77]
    extravagant, used
To eat long ago when Curius gathered
    with his own hands
Fresh greens from his little garden
    and cooked them on the brands
In his small fireplace—a dish that
    today is scorned at a glance
By a dirty ditchdigger in fetters,
    who remembers the taste
Of chitterlings in a reeking cookshop.
    Holidays were graced
In old times by a side of salt pork
    that hung in open racks;
Or they served a bacon flitch on
    family birthdays, with snacks
Of fresh meat added if a sacrificed
    beast should provide it.
A relation, already thrice hailed
    as consul, who once presided
As dictator of Rome and commanded
    armies, would shoulder the spade
With which he was taming mountainsides—
    by habit he stayed
Much later at work—and hurry home
    for a feast like that.
But when people quaked at the Fabii
    and stern Cato, or at

A Fabricius or Scaurus, when even
    rigid censors might fear
Their colleagues' harsh reproof, none
    thought it of any severe
Concern or a serious matter what kind
    of tortoiseshell
Was swimming in ocean abysses that
    could be used very well
On a fine, noble couch for Trojan-descended
    lords. Our beds
Never used to be oversized with
    inlaid frames; and the heads
Were simple—a bronze donkey face
    with garlands around the brows,
Beside which lusty farmboys were
    playing. Thus the house
Along with the furniture and the
    food were all of a piece.

[100] The rough soldier then hadn't
    learned to admire the arts of Greece,
And when, after cities were conquered,
    he got from the loot of wars
His share, he broke the cups of great
    artists so that his horse
Might rejoice in trappings, and his
    helmet, embossed, might show
A dying enemy scenes of the wolf mother,
    ordered to grow
Tame for the empire's future, the
    twin Quirini beneath
A ledge and naked Mars swooping down
    with spear and shield.
So their mush was served on clay
    plates; whatever silver they owned
Shone nowhere except on armor. All
    this, if you were prone
To the slightest envy, you'd envy. Also,
    the majesty

Of temples was closer around us then;
    and a voice could be
Heard in the midst of the city around
    midnight to say
The Gauls were marching from the
    seashore; and in this way
The gods took on themselves the
    office of prophecy.
Thus Jupiter warned us—such care
    for Latin affairs was he
Accustomed to bestow when his image
    in days of old
Was made out of clay and not defiled
    by any gold.

Those days saw us with tables   [117]
    homemade from our own trees;
The wood was at hand for this purpose
    if a storm from the east
By chance had toppled an old walnut.
    But today a rich man
Can't enjoy a dinner—venison, turbot,
    are tasteless, bland;
Perfumes and roses seem rancid—unless
    his broad table is laid
On a big solid-ivory leopard, with
    jaws wide open, made
Of tusks imported from Aswan's gates
    or lightfooted Moors
Or darker Hindus, or of those that
    mammoths shed in obscure
Arabian woods when too big and heavy
    for heads to sustain.
That's the secret of good appetite
    and digestion. For a plain
Table leg of silver to such as these
    is as bad as a brass
Ring on the finger. So I say to
    hell with this elegant class

Of society that would sniff in
    comparing its opulence
With my humble state. I haven't my
    first ounce of ivory since
My dice and draughts aren't made of
    it; and even my knives
Have handles of bone. Yet my lack
    taints nothing, never deprives
Any food of savor, nor makes it harder
    to cut the fowl.
But there'll be no carver to whom the
    whole school has to bow,
No student of Dr. Trypherus, who
    instructs in the art
Of carving with blunted knives and
    wooden models a smart,
Fine feast of sows' udders, hares,
    antelopes, flamingoes, boars,
Gaetulian gazelles, and pheasants
    until the whole outdoors
Is clattering with the elmwood banquet.
    My slave boy, a real
Novice and ignorant all his life,
    hasn't learned to steal
A slab of venison or a guinea hen's
    wing—he's had
No practice except in filching little
    scraps. A rough lad,
Well clothed to keep off the cold,
    will hand around plain cups,
Bought at the dime store. No Phrygian
    or Lycian boys, none bought up
At high prices from dealers will you
    find; if you should care
For something, ask in Latin! My boys
    dress alike; their hair,
Close cropped, has never been curled,
    and only today was combed
Because company's coming. One is a
    sturdy shepherd's son,

The other a cattle herder's; he sighs
    for the mother whom
He hasn't seen for so long, and is
    homesick, touched by gloom,
For the hut and the young goats he
    used to know—a boy who's got
An honest face and an artless modesty,
    just what
All those who are dressed in shining
    purple ought to be.
He doesn't have his armpits shaved
    and doesn't, when he
Is in the baths, like a juvenile
    delinquent, invite
Attention to his balls; he has nothing
    more to hide
His heavy private parts than an oil
    flask. He'll serve you wines
From the very hills where he was born,
    beneath whose pines
He played—for wine and server come
    from the same fatherland.

Perhaps you expect some Spanish   [162]
    damsels who get a hand
For indecent songs and dances sinking
    down to the floor
In a split with bottoms writhing—such
    things as brides adore
To see when sitting beside their
    husbands, but it would shame
Anyone to tell in their presence:
    the spur to lust, the same
Sharp sting that stirs the limber
    tools of rich men, brings forth
Even greater pleasure in the opposite
    sex: the more
It's prolonged, seducing eyes and
    ears, the sooner you'll wet

Yourself. My humble house offers no
    such nonsense. Let
Him listen to the clattering of
    castanets and words
A whore standing naked in her reeking
    crib would spurn,
Let him enjoy obscene cries and all
    of lechery's ways—
Him who slicks up his Lacedaemonian
    marble inlays
With wine spit out on the floor: for
    this in the rich we condone.
With middle-class people, adultery
    and gambling are known
As scandalous matters. But let those
    others do these same things
And we write them up in gossip
    columns—our playboy kings!
My feast today will provide a different
    pastime. We'll hear
The *Iliad* chanted, and Vergil's
    sublime epic poem, so near
Perfection it challenges the palm
    crown on Homer's head.
What does it matter with whose voice
    lines like these are read?

[183] So now forget business worries, don't
    talk shop, and take
A welcome day off. Enjoy doing
    nothing all day. And make
No mention of interest due, nor your
    wife, if she's the sort
To provoke your stifled anger by
    sneaking out to cavort
At dawn, returning at night with her
    fine gown wrinkled and wet
From lust, her hair disordered, her
    cheeks and ears burning yet.

Leave all your troubles before my
    threshold, cast off concern
For your house and slaves and things
    they lose or break or burn.
And above all, put aside all thoughts
    of thankless friends.

Right now the Megalesian games are   [193]
    here to attend—
Those solemn rites for Cybele—and
    in triumphal state
The praetor sits, the prey of horses
    he'll decimate,
And (if I may say it without offense
    to that vast crowd)
All Rome today is slave to the Circus.
    My ears with a loud
Uproar are struck, which tells me
    the emperor's team, the Green Sox,
Has won. For if it had lost, you'd
    see this city as shocked
And mournful as when our consuls
    fell in Cannae's dust.
Let young men watch who are better
    suited to shout and trust
Wild bets and sit with a smart girl
    there; let my shriveled skin
Drink the springtime sun and get out
    of my toga. Now, even when
It's an hour or more till noon, you
    may go to the baths—no disgrace
In being ahead of the crowd. You
    couldn't do this for five days
In a row because even such a life
    would become a bore:
When put to rarer use, our pleasures
    are prized much more.

XII

thanksgiving for a
shipwrecked friend

This day, Corvinus, is sweeter to
    me than my own birthday,
When altars of heaped green turf
    await the victims I'll slay,
As vowed to the gods. I'll offer a
    lamb with snow-white wool
To Queen Juno; one just as white to
    Minerva, in her full
Armor with Gorgons embossed; but for
    Jove this sacrifice,
A boisterous creature, bucking at
    the long halter, with eyes
Rolling around and head thrashing—for
    this is a fierce bull calf,
Ripe for temple and altar and sprinkling
    with wine. By now he's half
Weaned from his mother, ashamed to
    suck, and ready to scratch
The oaks with budding horns.
    If my means were great and could match
My desires, I'd haul up a bull much
    fatter than Hispulla, slow
From his very bulk. Not fed on
    neighboring pastures, he'd show
His pedigree from the finest stock
    of Clitumnus, would stride
Along to give his neck to a great
    priest's knife, and provide

The best offering for the return of
 my friend, still quaking, aghast
At the terrors lately endured and
 amazed to be safe at last.

For besides the perils the ocean   [17]
 holds, he escaped a stroke
Of lightning: a solid cloud, as
 thick and black as smoke,
Blotted out the sky, and a flashing
 fire struck suddenly down
On the yardarms. Each sailor imagined
 he was hit and soon
In horror thought that no shipwreck
 could ever compare
With a burning vessel. Everything
 happened exactly there,
And as frighteningly, as when a
 tempest arises in
A poem. But look, another kind of
 danger begins,
Just hear, and pity again,
 though the rest be the same as shown
Elsewhere—a terrible fate, indeed,
 but to many known
And one attested by votive tablets
 in many shrines.
Who doesn't know that Isis feeds
 these painters of signs?

My friend Catullus was hit by disaster   [29]
 just like these.
The hold was half full of water, the
 hull was pitched by high seas
From side to side, the gray-haired
 captain could bring no skill
To save the straining mast. And
 then—as a beaver will,

191

To save his life, castrate himself
        and part with those glands
He knows are sought for medicinal
        oil—Catullus began
To settle by jettison with the winds.
        "Heave all overboard,
All my cargo!" he cried, inclined
        to throw even his finest stores
To the sea, purple clothes just
        right for our spoiled Maecenases, too,
And others, which on the sheep's
        own backs were dyed their hue
By the nature of their excellent
        pastures, though it's clear
The secret virtues of water and
        air by the Guadalquivir
Do a lot to help. And when it came
        to the silver plate—
Salvers Parthenius made, three-gallon
        wine bowls fit to sate
The thirst of the centaur Pholus or
        Fuscus' wife—then he
Didn't hesitate: it was dumped, and
        with it went basketry,
And thousands of dishes, a whole set
        of goblets, highly wrought,
From which the cunning Philip of
        Macedon, who bought
Olynthus, had drunk. What other man
        now, anywhere on earth,
Would dare value his life above
        silver, safety above cash worth?
Some men make money not for the sake
        of living, but ache
In the blindness of greed and live
        just for their fortune's sake.

[52]   Now most of the cargo is overboard,
        but even this lack

Of weight is no help. So, faced
    with emergency, he fell back
On chopping down the mast to escape
    his perilous straits—
A poor last resort indeed when his
    only hope dictates
Reducing the ship! Go ahead, entrust
    to the winds your life,
To hewn planks that keep you three
    inches of pine—or maybe five,
If the ship is large—from death.
    Remember, next time take along,
In addition to your breadbasket,
    provisions, and that throng
Of potbellied flagons, some axes
    also to help in a storm!

When at last the sea calmed down,   [62]
    the sailors could perform
Their duties in better conditions.
    Destiny showed its command
Over winds and waves; and the joyful
    Fates, with kindly hand,
Spun a better thread of white wool.
    A wind, not much more strong
Than a gentle breeze, arose, and the
    lame ship sailed along
By only the makeshift device of
    clothes stretched out as sails
And a single canvas left at the prow.
    Soon the force of the gales
Abated, and hope of life, with the
    sun, returned. Into view
Then came the towering height so dear
    to Iulus, who
Preferred it to his stepmother's
    town, Lavinum, as home—
Mount Alba, named for that white sow
    whose wondrous womb

Cheered up the Trojan band with a
    sight never seen by it
Before: thirty piglets at thirty now
    world-famous tits!

[75]   At length the ship goes inside the
    moles erected to make
A harbor, past the Tyrrhenian lighthouse,
    the arms that break
The ocean's force, reaching out from
    Italy into the sea—
A port more wonderful, then, than any
    of nature's could be!
But the captain pilots his crippled
    ship to a berth inside,
A tranquil basin on which pleasure
    boats of Baiae may ride
Without danger. There the crew,
    with shaved heads now, but secure,
Enjoy recounting garrulous tales of
    perils endured.

[83]   Away with you, then, my boys—no
    talking, please; be pure
In heart. Garland the shrines, spread
    meal on the knives, adorn
The soft grass altars. I'll follow
    soon and when I've performed
The sacred rites which are principal
    here, I'll be homeward bound,
Where my little images, shining in
    fragile wax, will be crowned
With tiny wreaths. Here I'll appease
    great Jove, and light
Incense for my household gods and
    scatter pansies, bright
With all colors. Everything's shining!
    Because of this feast, my gate

Grows long laurel boughs and early-lit
    lanterns to celebrate!

But don't suspect my motives in this,   [93]
    Corvinus. For he,
Catullus, for whose return I build
    all these altars, has three
Small heirs of his own. You'll have
    to wait a rather long time
To find anybody who'd give a sickly
    hen, past her prime
And ready to close her eyes, for a
    friend so sure to fail
In making him rich. Why, a hen's
    too expensive! Not even a quail,
Not even that tiniest bird, will
    die for a man with an heir!
But if old Gallitta or Pacius, a
    rich and childless pair,
Begin to have fever, every foot of
    their porches will bloom
With tablets duly hung; there are
    some who'll vow hecatombs
For recovery, but merely of oxen—
    there's not a chance
Of finding on sale hereabouts a
    hundred young elephants,
Since nowhere in our Latin
    land has the creature bred,
But it's brought to us from the
    dusky nations and is fed
In the fields of Turnus and the
    Rutulian wood: Caesar's herd,
Trained to serve no commoner,
    since their ancestors were inured
To obey Tyrian Hannibal, our generals,
    and the king
Of Molossia and carry troops on
    their backs, no little thing

In war tactics, those armored towers
    lurching into the fray!
So Novius would not falter, nor would
    Pacuvius delay
To lead that huge walking ivory
    to the altar and slay
It for Gallitta's household
    gods: there's no victim bigger,
So none's more worthy of such gods
    and such gold diggers!
For the latter, if allowed, would
    vow to slay at a shrine
His tallest, handsomest slaves; on
    the girls' brows he would twine
Sacrificial bands—even on the boys.
    And if there should live
In his home a daughter ripe for
    marriage, then he would give
To the altar this Iphigenia—though
    hopeless beyond dispute
That a deer, dear to poets, would
    appear as a secret substitute.

[121] This fellow townsman I praise, and
    I don't compare a fleet
Of a thousand ships to a will. For
    if the patient cheat
The goddess of death, he'll be caught
    tight in a trap, destroy
His will, and rewarding truly marvelous
    service, employ
A few words to leave all, perhaps, to
    Pacuvius to enjoy,
Who then before his bested rivals may
    proudly strut.
You see, therefore, how well worthwhile
    a girl's throat cut
At Mycenae is! Long live Pacuvius—
    long enough to be

As old as Nestor, I pray! May he own
    such a quantity
Of riches as Nero stole. May he pile
    up gold by the ton
To mountainous heights. May he love
    no one and be loved by none!

XIII

ᎠᎬFᎡᎪUᎠᎬᎡS
anᎠ GUᎥLᎢY ᏟONSᏟᎥᎬNᏟᎬ

Anything a man does setting a bad
    example displeases
The doer himself. This is the first
    punishment that seizes
Upon him—no guilty man is acquitted
    if the judge
Is himself, although he may have
    won in court with a nudge
And a bribe to a venal justice who
    juggled the jury's votes.
What do you, Calvinus, think everyone
    is feeling about
This recent rooking you've had and
    your charge of breach of trust?
Yet you're not so poor this tiny hole
    in your income must
Drag you down to premature ruin;
    nor is it such a rare case.
Many men have had this misfortune;
    it's really a commonplace—
Just something that Fortune digs
    up from her ragbag. So quit
Your inordinate wailing. One's wrath
    shouldn't blaze more than is fit
And shouldn't exceed the loss. But
    you're hardly able to bear

The slightest touch of a small mishap
    and your guts now tear
And boil because your friend won't
    return the cash you consigned
To him on his sacred oath. And this
    you're surprised to find—
A man like you, even you, who'll
    never see sixty again,
Born when Fonteius was consul? You
    mean it was all in vain—
From all those years of experience
    you didn't learn one bit?

Indeed philosophy's great. It   [19]
    provides in its holy writ
The maxims to raise us over fortune.
    Still, we take the view
That they're happy too who learned
    in the school of life to make do
With all the discomforts and yet not
    chafe and fret at the yoke.
What day is so festal it fails to
    reveal some theft, some stroke
Of a master swindler or some embezzler—
    all manner of crime
For profit, and money got by poison
    or swords? It's a time
When honest men are scarce—hardly
    as many by count
As gates to Thebes or mouths of the
    fertile Nile. We live now
In a Ninth Age, more corrupt than the
    Age of Iron, and one
For whose vice even Nature can find
    no suitable name, for none
Of her metals is base enough. So we
    summon heaven and earth
To witness, as noisy as claques that
    give his money's worth

To Faesidius, cheering a speech.
    Tell me, you old man, who're
Most deserving of childhood's emblem,
    don't you know what allure
Other people's money has? Don't you
    know what a laugh you hand
To the rabble with your simplicity
    now when you demand
That anyone *not* break his oath and
    believe that gods reside
In temples or bloody altars? Primitive
    people have tried
Living thus in the past, before Saturn
    laid down his crown and fled
To take up a farmer's scythe, in the
    days when Juno led
The life of a maiden, and Jupiter
    still was a private man
In the caves of Mount Ida. Back
    then, no banquets ever were planned
In the sky for the gods—no Hebe; no
    Ganymede with wine bowls;
No Vulcan present, wiping his arms,
    begrimed by the coals
Of his island forge, and tossing
    off nectar. Each god used to dine
At home; there was not such a mongrel
    galaxy of the divine
Powers as we have today. The stars
    were content with a few
Divinities; thus with a lighter burden
    they didn't overdo
The load on poor Atlas. The lots hadn't
    yet been drawn to bestow
The dark underworld on a king. There
    was no stark, grim Pluto
With a wife from Sicily, no inexorable
    tortures, no wheel,
No rock, no Furies, no vultures;
    and the shades used to feel

Quite happy without a ruler below. In
    that bygone time,
Dishonesty was incredible. It was looked
    on as a crime,
Grievous, deserving death if a youth
    didn't rise from his seat
In the presence of elders, or if a
    boy didn't jump to his feet
Before any youth sprouting whiskers,
    though he himself might observe
In his own richer family home higher
    mounds of acorns served
And more strawberries. Four years'
    seniority was so revered,
And hallowed old age so equal the first
    thin fuzz of beard.

Today if a friend won't renege on   [60]
    money left in his trust
And returns the old purse with its
    rusty coins, his honesty's just
A marvel and worthy of the Etruscan
    scriptures, to be
Expiated by ewe lambs decked in
    garlands. If ever I see
An excellent, upright man—a freak,
    like a child that's born
Half beast, like pregnant mules or
    fishes dug up in the corn
By some astonished farmer's plow—I'm
    just as unnerved
As if it had rained down stones, or
    a swarm of bees had swerved
To settle upon the roof of a temple,
    or wondrous floods
Of milk were disgorged by a river to
    mix with the ocean's mud.

[71] You complain that five hundred dollars
        or so were taken from you
In an infamous fraud. What if someone
        else has lost from two
To ten thousand by this same underhand
        deal, and a third a sum
Still bigger, which in his huge
        strongbox could barely find room?
So simple and easy is it to scorn
        the witnessing gods
If no mortal man knows what was done.
        Just look with what
A loud voice he denies it and what
        an injured, innocent air
Lies on his treacherous face! By the
        rays of the sun, he swears,
By Jove's thunderbolts, the spear of
        Mars, the darts of the seer
Of Cirrha, the quiver and shafts of
        the virgin huntress, and then
By your own trident, O Neptune, lord
        of the Aegean's expanse;
He throws in Hercules' bow as well,
        and Minerva's lance,
And whatever weapons heaven's arsenals
        may supply.
In fact, if a father, he tearfully
        says: "May I, if I lie,
Eat my son's head boiled and served
        with Egyptian vinegar sauce!"

[86] Some men believe all things are
        ordained by the random toss
Of Fortune's dice, and the world
        is by no ruler controlled,
That changes of season, day and
        night, are by Nature unrolled;
And fearless, therefore, they'll
        touch altars anywhere, any time.

202

Another, although afraid that
    punishment follows a crime,
Though believing gods exist, will
    perjure himself just the same.
"Let Isis," he reasons, "do as she
    will with my body and claim
My sight with her vengeful sistrum
    so long as I keep the cash
I deny having stolen. It's worth
    being cursed with a putrid rash,
Tuberculosis, or cancer or losing a
    leg from gangrene.
If poor Ladas, the sprinter, didn't
    need a doctor to clean
Cobwebs from his brain by hellebore
    treatments, he'd never pause
At choosing gout and its riches.
    For what's the use of applause
Or Olympian olive wreaths for fast
    running? They're not good to eat!
Though the gods' wrath may be great,
    it's surely slow. If they mete
A penance to all guilty men, when on
    earth will they get to me?
But perhaps I may find the lenient
    god; he usually
Forgives these things. Men commit
    the same crime; fate smiles or frowns
To reward their wickedness—one gets
    a cross, another a crown."

That's the way they reassure their   [106]
    minds when terrified
By a guilty conscience. Then, call
    them to meet and swear inside
Some holy temple, they'll be there
    first—indeed, they're all set
To drag you there themselves and dare
    you to prove their debt.

For when a man shows a bold face to
    support a bad situation,
Many think he shows good faith.
    It's a fine acting job, a creation
Like that of the runaway clown in
    witty Catullus' play.
Poor fool, you may yell so loud that
    Stentor would yield the day,
Or as loudly as Homer's Mars: "Do
    you hear this, Jupiter, and not
Move your lips when you, whether
    made of bronze or marble, ought
To have spoken out? Else why do I,
    on your altar fires,
Put my opened pack of holy incense,
    a calf's liver slice,
Or cauls of pure white pigs? So far
    as I see, it's just
A tossup between your statues and
    shyster Vagellius' bust!"

[120] Hear what consolations in rebuttal
    a man may convey
Who hasn't adopted the Cynics' or
    Stoics' doctrines—they
Have only their shirts to keep them
    apart—who has low regard
For Epicurus, so pleased with the
    sprouts in his kitchen yard.
Diseases of doubtful prognosis should
    be healed by the best
Of specialists; but entrust your
    throbbing pulse to the test
Of a mere disciple of old Dr. Quack.
    If you can produce
In the whole wide world no crime so
    detestable as your abuse,
I'll hush and not forbid you to smite
    your breast with your fist

Or to slap your face since after so
    great a loss as this
You must close your doors, for a
    household mourns with greater distress
And louder wails the loss of money
    than loss by death.
In such an event no one's grief is
    feigned, no one is content
With rending only the hem of his
    clothes and squeezing a hint
Of tears from the corners of his eyes.
    For when a man hears
His money's lost, he doesn't pretend,
    he weeps genuine tears.

But if you see all courts overrun   [135]
    with complaints like yours,
If a bond, studied ten times by the
    claimant whom it insures,
Is called wastepaper and false, in
    spite of the signatures,
Handwriting, and seal on the ring—
    the finest sardonyx, cased
In an ivory box—do you imagine that
    you should be placed,
Dear fellow, beyond the common lot
    as though you were hatched
By a white hen, while we others are
    common chickens that scratched
Our way out of unlucky eggs? Your
    loss is a modest concern,
To be borne with modest amounts of
    spleen if only you turn
Your eyes upon worse crimes. Compare
    it with robbers for hire,
Or sulfur lighted by a device and
    your threshold afire
With bursting flames. Think also of
    those who steal from old

Temples the splendid cups whose very
    rust we should hold
In reverence, nations' gifts, or
    crowns ancient kings bestowed.
If these aren't there, a second-rate
    sacrilegious thief
Turns up to scrape from the thigh of
    Hercules the gold leaf,
Or shave even Neptune's face, or peel
    off Castor's gold.
And why should he hesitate who
    usually melts down a whole
Jupiter, lightning and all? Think
    also about the men
Who mix and sell black poisons, the
    parricide sewn in the skin
Of an ox and cast in the ocean, with
    him, through adverse fate,
An ape that harmed no one. What a
    fraction, these, of the spate
Of crimes the city's prefect, Gallicus,
    hears from the day's
First light till it fades! If you'd
    know the ways of the human race,
That one courthouse will be enough.
    Spend a few days there,
And when you come out, call yourself
    unfortunate if you dare!
Who's ever surprised at goiters in
    the Alps, or breasts
On a woman in Meroë bigger than her
    fat babe? Who suggests
It's amazing to see yellow-haired,
    blue-eyed Germans who wind
Their pomaded locks into horns? No
    one; for that's the kind
Of creatures they are. To fight off
    attacks of Thracian cranes
That suddenly swoop in a clamorous
    cloud, the pygmy campaigns

With his tiny weapons; but soon,
    unevenly matched with his foes,
He's caught by the savage bird and
    carried in crooked claws
Through the air. If you saw this
    here among our people, you'd shake
With laughter; but there, though these
    same fights are constantly faced,
No one laughs where the whole army
    isn't more than one foot high.

"Will this perjured man and infamous   [174]
    fraud not be punished by
The law?" Suppose he were rushed
    off in heavy shackles and
At our pleasure slain—what more
    could your anger demand?
But still you've lost your money;
    you'll never hold in your hand
The deposit you gave him. The
    tiniest drop of blood that falls
From his headless body will bring,
    with its solace, hatred and gall.
"But revenge is good, sweeter than
    life itself!" To be sure,
The stupid think so; you'll see
    their hearts blaze up for obscure
And paltry reasons, often for none
    at all; indeed,
No matter how small the occasion be,
    it's all they need
For anger. Chrysippus won't say the
    same, nor gentle Thales,
Nor the old man who lived near
    honeyed Hymettus, Socrates,
Who would give to his accuser no
    portion of the contents
Of the hemlock cup brought during his
    cruel imprisonment.

Sweet Wisdom gradually strips from
    us most vices, all error,
First teaching what's right. For
    revenge is always the joy of narrow,
Sick, and petty minds. Take as proof,
    right off, what this shows:
No one so dotes on revenge as
    a woman.

[192]   But why suppose
Such men have gone scot-free whose
    minds are constantly gripped
By terror, fully aware of their evil
    deeds, who are whipped
By blows unheard, whose consciences
    brandish over their heads
An unseen scourge of torture?
    Moreover, it is a dread
Punishment, far more cruel than those
    contrived by severe
Caedicius or Rhadamanthus, both day
    and night to bear
In your breast your own accuser.
    The Pythian priestess replied
To a Spartan once that in time to
    come he could never hide
From punishment, seeing that he had
    thought to keep as his
A sum in his trust and defend the
    fraud by perjury—this
Because he was asking what the deity's
    mind might be
And whether Apollo would advise him
    to do this deed.
Therefore he restored the money, but
    out of fear, not through
His honesty. Still he found all the
    oracle's words were true

And worthy of the shrine; for he,
   his family, and kin,
However distant, were all destroyed.
   The mere wish to sin
Incurs such penalties. For he who
   secretly plots
In his heart any crime is guilty of
   the deed.

            Then what   [210]
If he does what he planned? His
   anxiety never ends; it intrudes
Even on his meals; his throat is dry
   as if fevered; his food
Is stubborn, swelling between his
   teeth; but the poor wretch spits
The wine out, can't bear the choicest
   old Alban vintage, and sits,
If you bring something finer, with
   deep wrinkles gathering on his brow,
As though puckered up at some Falernian
   wine gone sour.
At night, if his worries by chance
   allow him to sleep for an hour,
And his limbs, after tossing about
   on the bed, are now at ease,
At once the temple, the altar, the
   god he outraged, he sees,
And what racks his mind with special
   pangs, sees you in nightmares:
Your awesome figure, larger than life,
   alarms him and scares
A confession from him. These are the
   men who shake and turn pale
At each lightning flash; at the first
   dim rumble from heaven they quail,
When it thunders they faint—as
   though storms weren't accidental or bred

By raging winds, but a flame of wrath
    flung down on the head
Of man in judgment. If one storm
    pass without harm, they dread
The next one more anxiously, as though
    this calm would gain
Them only a short reprieve. Further,
    if they suffer a pain
In the side with fever allowing no
    sleep, they think the disease
Was sent on their flesh by an angry
    deity; they think these
Are stones and spears of the gods.
    Bleating lambs they dare not vow
To a shrine, nor crested cocks to the
    Lares. For what hope is allowed
Sick, guilty men? Or what victim is
    not more worthy than they
To live? The nature of wicked men
    is almost always
Fickle and shifty. When they're
    committing a crime, they teem
With courage; only after it's done
    do they start to feel
What's right and wrong. Yet nature,
    firm and unable to change,
Returns to its old condemned ways.
    For who has ever placed
A limit to his misdeeds? When have
    blushes, once put aside,
Returned to a vice-hardened face?
    What man who was satisfied
With a single crime have you seen?
    Our con man will get his feet
In a trap and suffer the hook in a
    murky jail or a seat
On a rock isle in the Aegean Sea,
    whose crags are packed

Already with famous exiles. Then
    you will rejoice in the fact
That a hated name is bitterly punished,
    and happily find
At last that the gods aren't deaf nor,
    like Tiresias, blind.

XIV

evil precedents
set by parents

Many things have sinister reputations,
    Fuscinus—such things
As stain the brightest promise with
    evil darkness that clings
Through life—which parents themselves
    reveal and pass on to sons.
If old daddy likes ruinous gambling,
    his heir also has begun
In his teens and rattles the same
    weapons in his junior dicebox.
Nor need his kin hope for better of
    any stripling who shocks
Them all by peeling his truffles,
    spicing mushrooms, and next
By sousing ortolans with rich sauce—
    all learned from the text
Of a gluttonous throat his spendthrift
    father taught. By the time
He's seven, with baby teeth still
    in his jaws, you may call the prime,
Bearded tutors, a thousand on this
    side, as many on that, but still
He'll always crave fine dinners with
    sumptuous menus and will
Not let gourmet standards degenerate
    in his *haute cuisine.*

Is Rutilus teaching the ways of a   [15]
    gentle spirit, serene
In temper, kind to small faults?
    Does he think that slaves have bone
And flesh and souls created of
    substance as good as our own?
Or is he teaching cruelty, with his
    delight in the sound
Of a savage flogging—a music that
    holds him more spellbound
Than that of the Sirens? Tyrant and
    giant, Antiphates rolled
Into one with Polyphemus, to browbeat
    his trembling household,
He can only be happy when the
    torturer comes in to brand
Someone with hot irons for two
    missing napkins. In what does a man
Instruct his son when he thrills at
    clanking chains and warms
With excessive pleasure at branded
    slaves and prison farms
And dungeon cells? Are you such a
    simpleton you think
The daughter of Larga will not become
    an adulterous minx,
Who never could count so quickly her
    mother's lovers' names
Or reel them all off with so much
    speed that it wasn't a strain
To finish before she took thirty
    breaths? Her mother's games
Were known to the child, who now
    inscribes, as Mommy dictates,
Her own little love notes and sends
    them to her chosen bedmates
By the same fairy messengers. Thus
    Nature ordains. Home-grown

Examples of evil corrupt us more
    quickly since they set a known
And revered authority over our minds.
    Perhaps one or two
Young men may resist whose souls
    Prometheus formed with more true,
Loving care and a finer clay. But
    the rest are led on to follow
Their fathers' steps, which should
    be shunned, and dragged down to wallow
Along that worn path of vice so often
    portrayed to them.

[38] Therefore avoid all things that you
    know you must condemn.
There's at least one urgent reason
    for this: that our children not
Imitate our crimes. For we're all
    quite ready to be taught what
Is wicked and wrong. You can turn
    up a Catiline here or there
In any tribe, but you won't find a
    Brutus or Cato anywhere.
Where a father lives, no filthy word
    or sight should cross
The threshold. Away, away with you
    all, you girls who are bossed
By a pimp and you parasites who sing
    the whole night through!
If you plan some vile affair, your
    deepest reverence is due
Your son; and don't make light of his
    age—let your infant son
Prevent you from the intended sin.
    For if he should run
Up against the censor's ire some day
    for something he's done,
And turns out to be like you, not
    only in figure and face

But a chip off the old block in vice,
    who followed you pace by pace
Into viler sins than your own, of
    course you'll upbraid him and rant
And rage, and later plan to change
    your will. But you can't
Assume the scowl and the rights of
    a parent, can you, when you
In old age are doing worse things,
    and for a long time, too,
The windy cupping glass at your
    brainless head has probed?

With a guest expected, none in your   [59]
    house is idle. "Sweep the floor,
Clean the columns, wipe down that
    dried-up spider and all
The web! Here, shine the plain silver;
    you there, the embossed bowls!"
The master blusters, urging them on
    and gripping a lash.
So you fear, poor fool, a pile of
    dog dung in the hall or a splash
Of mud on the porch may offend the
    eyes of your coming friend.
And yet with a pail of sawdust one
    slave boy cleans what offends.
But do you not trouble yourself that
    your son may set his eyes
On a virtuous home without any stain
    and free from vice?
It's fine that you've added a citizen
    to our population
And country, if you rear him to be
    worthwhile to the nation,
Of use to farms and what we in war
    and peace undertake.
For the morals and habits in which
    you bring him up will make

The greatest difference. Storks feed
    their babies on the snakes
And lizards found in remote wild
    fields; and when they succeed
On their wings, the young hunt those
    same animals. Vultures speed
From dead cattle and dogs and corpses
    on gibbets to bring a piece
Of carrion to their young, so this
    is the food of these
Now grown-up vultures, feeding
    themselves as they build their nests
In trees of their own. And the noble
    birds that await the behest
Of Jove hunt hares or kids in the
    forest and bring this prey
To their eyries; so when the mature
    offspring can fly away,
Their hunger moves them to swoop on
    that same prey as well
That they had tasted first after
    pecking out of their shells.

[86]   Cretonius loved construction; and now
    on the crooked strand
Of Gaeta, now on Tivoli's highest
    peaks, now on land
In Praenestine hills, he used to build his
    high-roofed grand
Mansions, with marble brought from
    Greece and farther, to tower
Above the temples of Fortune or Hercules,
    just as our
Own Capitol House was outdone by
    Posides, the eunuch. Thanks,
Therefore, to living in that fashion,
    Cretonius shrank
His estate and hurt his fortune;
    still, it wasn't a small

Amount he left. His demented son
    then squandered it all
To build new mansions of even more
    costly marble blocks.

Some men who chance to be born of a   [96]
    father who's orthodox
In keeping the Sabbath worship nothing
    but clouds and a kind
Of unseen God in the heavens. No
    difference to their minds
In pig flesh, from which the father
    abstained, and human; then
They're soon circumcised. But accustomed
    to scorn Roman laws, they begin
To study and practice and revere
    Jewish law and also
What Moses handed down in his secret
    book—not to show
The road to any who worships rites
    that are not the same;
To lead only bobtailed men to the
    longed-for fountain. But blame
Falls on the father to whom each
    seventh day was a day
Of sloth and had no concern with life
    in any way.

However, the young imitate most vices   [107]
    of their own
Accord; they're forced against their
    will to avarice alone.
For here's a vice that seems and
    looks like virtue; it deceives
Because it has a gloomy demeanor and
    unrelieved
Severity of expression and dress.
    The miser is praised,

Without doubt, as thrifty, a man who
    saves for rainy days,
Who'll keep safer guard on his wealth
    than would—if they policed
The same—the dragons of Colchis or
    the Hesperides.
In addition, this man I speak of is
    thought shrewd in the art
Of making money, for through these
    coinsmiths, fortunes start
To grow, but they grow by devious
    means and always increase:
The anvil's always clanking; fires
    in the forge never cease.

[119] From this the father judges that
    misers are happy as kings;
And so, if he worships wealth, believing
    there's no such thing
As a poor but contented man, he
    exhorts his sons to embark
Upon that course and study in that
    same school. There are
Certain rudiments in vice; he imbues
    them from the start
In these and compels them to learn
    the pettiest stingy arts;
At length he teaches insatiable lust
    for acquiring wealth.
He shrinks slaves' bellies with short
    rations, and he himself
Goes hungry too, for he never can
    bear to eat all the stale bread,
Now blue with mold. In midsummer's
    heat, he'll save up a shred
Of yesterday's hash and store for
    tomorrow's dinner some beans
Left over, a mackerel head or half
    a stinking sardine

With slices of leek, which he counts
    before he lets them go.
Ask a beggar on any bridge to a meal
    like that, he'll say no!
But why do you suffer torments like
    these to pile up a mass
Of wealth, when obviously it's crazy—
    sheer madness—to pass
Your life in poverty just so you'll
    be rich when you die?
Meanwhile, as your coffers fill,
    overflow, and multiply,
Your love of wealth grows as great
    as the wealth itself has grown.
For the man who has none covets it
    least. The one house you own
Out of town isn't good enough—you
    buy another. Next door
The cornfields seem bigger and better
    than yours; then you deplore
Your cramped domain. You buy them
    too, and others with these—
Woods, vineyards, and hills thick with
    gray-bloomed olive trees.
If the owner won't budge, regardless
    of your price, you might
Send a herd of lean, starving oxen,
    with weary necks, by night
Into his sprouting corn, and they
    won't return to the stall
Till the whole new crop is in their
    ravenous bellies. You'd call
It a clean sweep by a sickle. The
    number can hardly be told
Of those bewailing such wrongs, or
    of fields this outrage has sold.

But what talk, what horn blasts of   [152]
    evil gossip there will be!

"What's the harm in that? Much better
    I rake in the lettuce," says he,
"Than the praise of the whole countryside
    for reaping the meager yield
Of a tiny farm." Of course! And
    you'll be immune to disease
And old age, you'll have no troubles,
    no sorrow, and you'll rate
A much longer span of life and henceforth
    a rosier fate
If only *you only* possess all the acres
    of farmland plowed
By the Romans when Tatius reigned!
    In later times we allowed
Our veterans, broken with age and the
    trials of Punic wars
Or dread Pyrrhus and his Molossian
    swords, for all their scars
And wounds a bonus at last of hardly
    two acres of ground.
None ever thought this reward too
    small for service that bound
Them to toil and blood, or shabby
    thanks from a stingy homeland.
Such a farm was ample to feed the
    father himself and his band
Of young at the house, where his
    wife lay big with child and four
Small children played—three his own and on
    slave-born. What's more,
For their big brothers, back from
    work in the fields, a hot
Second, heartier meal of porridge
    steaming in a huge pot
Would be ready. Today we couldn't
    imagine such a small plot
Of ground as really sufficient to
    make a garden for us!

Therein lies the cause of most crime: [173]
    No vice is a stimulus
To mixing more poisoned bowls or
    plunging so often the sword
As the fierce desire for unbounded
    wealth. For he who would hoard
Great wealth would do it quickly.
    But what respect for law,
What fear or shame does a hurrying
    miser ever know?
"Live content with these small homes
    and hills of yours, my sons,"
The Marsian, Hernican, and Vestinian
    fathers once
Said long ago. "Let us get our food
    by the plow and the spade—
Enough for our tables. Our rustic
    gods approve it; their aid
And kindness brought us the welcome
    gift of grain and made
Man loathe his ancient acorn diet.
    The man who is not
Ashamed to wear high boots in the
    snow, who keeps off the onslaught
Of the cold East Wind by skins with
    the fur inside, will never
Wish to commit a forbidden act.
    Purple cloth, whatever
It be—foreign and unknown to us—
    leads to vice and crime."

Such counsel these ancients gave [189]
    their children. But in our time,
After autumn a father rouses his
    sleeping son with a shout
In the midnight hours: "Wake up,
    my boy, get to work, write out
Your notes, draw up your briefs, read
    all the red-lettered laws

Of our sires, or request a centurion's
    post. But see that you cause
Commander Laelius to notice your
    uncombed head, also your
Hairy nostrils, and admire your bulging
    arms. Raid the Moors'
Small huts and Brigantes' forts so
    that at sixty you'll get
The eagle emblem—and riches! Or if
    you can't stand the sweat
And hard work of camps, if the sound
    of bugle and trumpet compel
Your bowels to move, start trading—
    buy something you can sell
At fifty per cent pure profit. Don't
    be too snobbish to enter
A trade that has to be banished away
    from the city's center
And over the Tiber. Don't try to
    sniff out distinctions between
A perfume shop and a tannery; the
    smell of profit is clean
And sweet, whatever the source. Let
    this maxim always be
On your lips—one worthy of the gods
    and even, if he
Were a poet, of Jupiter himself:
    "Nobody asks where
You get it, but money you have to
    have." This is what spare,
Old, shriveled nurses teach little
    boys still crawling; these
Are the things that every girl learns
    before her ABC's.

[210]   To the father eager to teach such
          precepts, no matter who,
      I'd say this: "Tell me, you stupid
          ass, who orders you

To hurry? The pupil, I'll bet, will
    excel the master. So quit
And don't worry. You'll be surpassed,
    as Telamon had to submit
To Ajax, his son, as Peleus was by
    Achilles outdone.
Be patient with young people; their
    bones haven't yet begun
To fill with the marrow of full-fledged
    evil. When he starts to feel
A fuzz on his cheeks and shave with
    a razor's edge, then he'll
Give false testimony and sell his
    perjuries for a small sum
While touching Ceres' altar and foot.
    If there should come
A daughter-in-law with a fatal dowry
    through your door,
Consider her buried already. What
    fingers will squeeze her throat
While she's fast asleep! For all the
    riches that you expect
To be gained by trade on land and
    sea, your son will collect
By a shorter route; indeed, great
    crimes take no effort. Some day
You'll say, 'I never taught these
    things, nor advised such ways.'
And yet the cause, the origin, of his
    wrongdoings lies
In you. For whoever teaches the
    love of wealth, by sly
And sinister lessons turns his sons
    into misers; and he
Who gives a son freedom to double
    bequests by fraud, gives free
Rein to his impetus. Call him back,
    he can't stop or turn round,
And despising you, hurries on,
    stampeding out of bounds.

Nobody's satisfied with sinning just
    so much as you
Allow—so much broader the self-
    indulgence they pursue!

[235] "When you tell a youth, a man's a
    fool who gives to a friend
Or helps relieve the impoverished
    state of one of his kin,
You teach him to plunder, to cheat,
    by any crime to acquire
More riches, the love of which stirs
    you with as great a fire
As the love of country did the hearts
    of the Decii, as deep—
If we can believe those Greeks—as
    that of Menoeceus for Thebes,
That land whose furrows, sown with
    dragons' teeth, sprang to life
With legions of men in arms, who fell
    into horrible strife
At once, as though a bugler tootling
    alarms had been raised
Also from the earth with them. Therefore,
    you will see the blaze
Whose sparks you kindled yourself
    now raging far and wide
And sweeping all before it. And don't
    think your own wretched hide
Will be spared! Your pupil, the lion
    cub, with hideous roars
Will gobble his trembling master in
    his den. Of course,
Astrologers know your horoscope; but
    it's tiresome to wait
For a slow-turning spindle, and you'll
    die with your thread of fate
Not yet snapped. Already you stand
    in his way and thus postpone

His ambitions, and your long and
    staglike old age has thrown
The boy into torment. Get Dr. Archigenes
    quickly and buy
The draft Mithridates compounded.
    And if you expect to try
Another fig or to pick another rose,
    you should drink
Before meals the antidote of a man
    who's both father and king."

I'll show you now the choicest of   [256]
    entertainments, one that
No theater, no games put on by a
    praetor, however rich,
Can match if you'll observe at what
    risk to life men attain
Increase of wealth, much money in
    brassbound chests, or coins
That must go for deposit with
    vigilant Castor now that Mars
The Avenger was robbed of even his
    helmet and couldn't guard
His own treasure. And so you may give
    up all the curtains of shows
That honor Cybele, Flora, and Ceres;
    the games that expose
Real people's affairs are so much
    better. Is there more the mind
Can enjoy in tumblers, trapeze artists,
    men sliding down inclined
Tightropes—or in you, whose whole
    life is spent being tossed
On a merchant vessel by winds from
    north or south, quite lost
To common sense, a low trader in smelly
    cargo and sweet,
Thick wine you love to import from
    the shores of ancient Crete,

With flagons made in Jove's birthplace—
    fellow-citizens, say?
But the man who dares set foot on a
    rope and on it can stay
In balance derives a living thereby;
    he's safe against cold
And hunger. But you walk a tightrope,
    hoping for millions in gold
And a hundred villas. Look at our
    ports, our seas packed close
With massive ships: more men now
    work on the ocean than those
On shore. A fleet will appear to
    take you wherever a chance
Of profit beckons, not only will
    cross the broad expanse
Of Carpathian and Gaetulian waters,
    but will advance,
Leaving Calpe far behind, through
    the Pillars of Hercules,
To hear the setting sun hissing
    in western seas.
It's well worth your pains that you,
    having faced the half-grown mermen
And monsters of the deep, return
    home safe to determine
The wealth in your bulging purse
    and exult in fat moneybags!

[284] There's more than just one kind of
    madness. Orestes sags
In his sister's arms, is terrified
    by the look and the flames
Of the Furies; Ajax, killing a ox,
    believes that famed
Agamemnon or Ulysses bellows. The
    man who has stored
His ship to the gunwales with goods,
    with only a width of board

Between him and the water, needs a
    keeper—not that he rips
His cloak and tunic apart, but
    because he bears such hardships
And danger for bits of silver incised
    with little faces
And titles. It clouds up and thunders—
    the trader who bought up cases
Of pepper or grain cries, "Weigh anchor!
    A sky that color, that wall
Of black clouds, are nothing to be
    feared. Heat lightning, that's all!"
Perhaps the poor fool on this very
    night will be washed overboard,
As the hull breaks up, be engulfed
    by waves, and clutch his adored
Moneybelt in one hand or in his teeth.
    Yesterday all the gold
The Tagus and yellow Pactolus roll in
    their sands wouldn't hold
His desires in check; but today he's
    glad of some rags to cheat
The cold at his naked loins, and some
    scraps of food to eat,
While he, shipwrecked, begs pennies,
    and with the painted storm
That sank his vessel hung on his breast,
    looks to it for support.

Anything got by such woes is   [303]
    preserved by still greater care
And fear: to guard a great fortune
    is irksome. The millionaire
Licinus orders a troop of slaves to
    stand watch all night
With fire buckets ready, as he fears
    for his amber, his white
Statues and Phrygian marbles, ivory
    and tortoiseshell plaques.

The tub of the naked Cynic doesn't
    get burned. If you crack
And break it, he'll make a new home
    next day, or patch it with nails.
Alexander, when he beheld this tub's
    great host, didn't fail
To sense how much happier this man
    was, who had no desires,
Than he who must possess for himself
    the world entire
And go on to suffer dangers as great
    as his enterprise.
O Fortune, you'd have no divine attributes
    if we were wise:
It's we who make you a goddess!

[316]   But if anyone asks me
What amount of wealth is enough,
    I'll answer: As much as may be
Required by thirst and hunger and
    cold; as much as sufficed
For you, Epicurus, in your small
    garden; as much as comprised
The needs of the house of Socrates
    in an earlier day.
Nature never says one thing, Wisdom
    another. You say
I seem to restrict you with examples
    too harsh and grim?
Then add something from our modern
    ways; get enough to swim
Up to the rank that Otho's law declared
    worth a seat
In the fourteen rows. If that too
    makes you frown and pout, compete
For two knighthoods, even three—thrice
    twenty thousand dollars!
If I haven't yet filled your lap,
    if it still has gaping hollows,

Not the wealth of Croesus or Persian
    kings can ever presume
To sate your greed, nor even the
    wealth of Narcissus, on whom
Claudius Caesar lavished every fortune
    and whose will
He obeyed when, though it was his wife,
    ordered to kill.

εgγptian cannibals

Who doesn't know, Volusius, friend
    from Bithynia, the kinds
Of monsters the mad Egyptians worship?
    One district enshrines
The crocodile, another reveres the
    ibis that fills
Its belly with snakes, and where the
    magical music trills
From broken Memnon, and ancient
    Thebes with its hundred gates
Lies ruined, the gold idol of a
    sacred longtailed ape
Is shining. In one place, cats,
    in another catfish, and whole
Cities pray to a dog, but no one to
    Diana. They hold
It a sin to injure onions and leeks
    by taking a bite.
What a pious race, for whom these
    gods are brought forth right
In their gardens! No woolbearing
    beast may be served at any meal,
It's unlawful there to slaughter a
    she-goat's kid—but to feed
On the flesh of a man is allowed!
    When Ulysses told of a deed
Like this to amazed Alcinous at a
    banquet, he stirred

Some to rage, or laughter perhaps,
    as a vagrant liar. "Absurd!
Is none of us going to throw this
    fellow into the sea,
Who deserves a fierce and real
    Charybdis, seeing that he
Invented monstrous Laestrygones and
    Cyclopes? For I
Would sooner believe in Scylla, the
    clashing rocks that lie
In the Bosporus, skins full of storms,
    or that Elpenor and his
Shipmates, when touched by Circe's
    thin wand, became grunting pigs.
Did he think us Phaeacians so
    empty-headed and asinine?"
So someone might justly have spoken
    who only a little wine
Had taken from the Corcyraean pitcher
    and wasn't yet drunk.
For Ulysses had none to swear his
    tales were not pure bunk.

Now I will tell of wonderful strange   [27]
    events that all
Took place just lately, when Juncus
    was consul, beyond the walls
Of tropical Coptus—a crime of the
    common people and worse
Than any found in tragedies; for
    though you search every verse
Of the drama from Pyrrha's time
    till today, you'll find no crime
Committed by a whole people. But
    listen to what a prime
Example horrible savagery in our day
    has produced.

[33] An ancient, long-nourished feud, an
      undying hatred no truce
Can resolve, and wounds that can't
      be healed, are burning between
The neighboring towns of Ombi and
      Tentyra. Each side is seen
Swelling up with fury because each
      one has always hated
Its neighbor's gods and believed
      that none should be venerated
As gods but its own. So when a
      festival time came around,
The leaders and chiefs of the enemy
      cult thought they had found
A good chance that shouldn't be
      missed to keep the other town
From enjoying a glad and happy day—
      great feasts in squares
And temples on the tables, and
      sofas that got constant wear
From lollers day and night, till
      the sun for the seventh time rose
To surprise them. Egypt is, no doubt,
      uncouth; but in those
Debaucheries practiced today, from
      what I myself have seen,
Its barbaric mob yields nothing to
      ill-famed Canopus. They dream
That defeat of babbling, staggering
      drunks would not be hard.
Over there men dancing to a black
      piper, with nard or lard
Or heaven knows what and flowers
      and chaplets on their heads;
Over here, a ravening hate. But
      they start, with noise widespread,
Their first insults—war trumpets
      to passions burning to fight.
Then shouts back and forth, they
      clash, and bare hands rage to smite

Instead of weapons. Few jaws and
    chins escape being gashed,
Few noses, or none, come out of the
    fracas unbloodied, unsmashed.
Throughout the ranks can be seen
    broken faces, looking like none
That's human, bones gaping through
    torn cheeks, and fists that run
With blood from eyes. Yet they
    think themselves at play, in a game
Of waging war, like boys, for no
    corpses are trampled in shame.
And indeed, to what end does a mob
    of so many thousands brawl
If everyone lives? So the fight
    grows fiercer, and now they fall
To throwing stones—the usual weapon
    in riots—which they,
Stooping down, search for on the
    ground: and not such stones as weigh
Like those which Turnus or Ajax threw,
    or Diomedes
Struck on the hip of Aeneas, but
    such as right hands like these
We have today, so different from
    theirs, may be able to cast.
For even when Homer lived, this
    race was declining fast.
The earth now brings forth weak,
    wicked men; and therefore, after
Some god has seen them, he's moved
    to only loathing and laughter.

But enough of digressions; back to   [72]
    my tale! At last one side
Gets armed reinforcements and boldly
    draws its swords and strides
With barrages of deadly arrows to
    start the battle again.

The men who live on nearby Tentyra's
     palm-shaded plain
Turn their backs in fearful panic
     before the Ombite attack.
Now one, too scared and rushing, trips
     up and is caught. They hacked
His body to thousands of bits and
     pieces so that one gob
Of the dead man might go to each man
     in the conquering mob.
And they ate him up, bones and all,
     not waiting to stew up a pot
Or roast him on spits. It took so
     long to get a fire hot,
They felt—so boring to wait! They
     ate the corpse raw and still warm!

[84] We may take some joy at least that
     sacred fire, which the arm
Of Prometheus stole from highest heaven
     and gave the nations
Of earth, was not defiled there. I
     offer congratulations
To that element, and think you rejoice.
     But never was flesh
So gladly devoured as by him who
     could bear to chew that fresh
Cadaver. But do not doubt, don't
     even ask, in an act
Of such horror, if only the first
     throat felt delight. For in fact,
With the corpse now wholly eaten,
     the last to come up stood
Smearing fingers over the ground to
     get a taste of the blood.

[93] The Vascones, it is said, once prolonged
     their lives by eating

Such food; but that was a different
    case. They'd taken a beating
In war, and adverse fortune
    brought on the final distress
Of famine imposed by an endless siege.
    The wretchedness
Of the people just named, in having
    to turn to such food, should call
Forth our pity, for not till every
    green leaf, every animal,
And anything else that the pangs of
    empty bellies condemn
Men to eat, so that even their enemies
    pitied their wizened limbs,
Their pallor and gauntness—not until
    then did they, in complete
Starvation, tear the limbs of others,
    when ready to eat
Even their own. For what man or what
    god would refuse to grant
A pardon to bellies that suffered
    such horrid, inhuman demands,
When even the souls of the dead might
    forgive those who were brought
To eating their bodies. Much better
    by Zeno are we taught:
For some things must be done to preserve
    our lives, he thought,
Though indeed not everything. But
    how could Spaniards be Stoics,
Especially in times of ancient
    Metellus? Today a heroic
Athens may still be in Greece, but
    there's one in Rome as well,
And all over the world. Those eloquent
    Gauls have begun to sell
Instructions to British lawyers, and
    Iceland has plans now aimed
At hiring a rhetorician. And yet
    these people I've named

Were noble; and those of Saguntum,
    their equals in loyalty
And courage but more than equal in
    slaughter, make the same plea
For excuse. But Egypt's more savage
    than the dread altar found
On the Sea of Azov; for if you think
    what old poets hand down
Is trustworthy, the Tauric Diana
    who founded the grim rite slays
Only strangers; the victim has nothing
    further, no disgrace
Worse than the knife, to fear. But
    what distress drove this race
Of Egyptians? What raging famine or
    armies besieging the walls
Forced them to dare so horrid and
    monstrous a thing? If all
The lands of Memphis were parched and
    dry, could they devise
Any other outrage to the Nile for
    being unwilling to rise?
No wild Cimbrians or Britons, no
    savage Scythians or dread
Agathyrsians ever so rabidly raged as
    this rabble, afraid
Of war and useless, that hoists baby
    sails on crockery fleets
And rows painted pottery boats with
    puny oars! You can mete
Out no penalty proper for such a
    crime, no punishment frame
For people in whose minds anger and
    hunger are one and the same.
Nature, in giving tears to man,
    confessed that he
Had a tender heart; this is our
    noblest quality.
Therefore she makes us weep for the
    anguish of friends arraigned

For trial, pleading their cause, or
    a ward whose sex isn't plain
From tear-streaming cheeks and
    girlish hair who summons to high
Court a defrauder. At Nature's behest
    we grieve and sigh
When the bier of a maiden, full-grown
    and never wed, goes by,
Or when earth closes over a babe too
    young for the funeral pyre.
For what good man, one worthy to
    hold up the mystic fire
Of Ceres' torch, one such as her
    priest would want him to be,
Believes he's untouched by any
    other's adversity?
Compassion distinguishes us from
    dumb brutes; so we alone,
Who have been endowed with a nature
    deserving respect, who own
The genius for godlike deeds, are
    fit to cultivate
And use the arts, have drawn from
    highest heaven those traits
Of donated feeling denied to lowly
    beasts with gaze bowed
To the ground. At the world's
    beginning our common creator allowed
Only life to them. But to us he gave
    soul as well, that love
For each other might stir us to ask
    or offer aid; to move
From ancient forests and groves where
    our forefathers lived; to draw
The scattered cave-dwellers together
    and form a nation in law;
To build homes and join others to
    our own, so neighboring doors,
From trust born of our union, might bring
    safe sleep; with force

Of arms to protect a fellow-citizen
    when he falls
Or reels from a huge and grievous
    wound; to sound battle calls
On one common trumpet, with our common
    defense to be
The same city walls, behind gates
    locked by a single key.

[159] But today there's more fellowship
    among snakes than among mankind.
Wild beasts spare those with similar
    markings. When can you find
The stronger lion killing the weaker?
    In what wood has a boar
Ever died by the tusks of a bigger
    boar? The tigers that roar
In India live in continual peace
    together; the rough
Wild bear gets along with other wild
    bears. But it isn't enough
For man to have forged on unholy
    anvils our deadly blades.
The first blacksmiths, accustomed to
    forge only rakes and spades
And exhaust themselves making hoes
    and plowshares, never knew
How to beat out swords. We now see
    a people whose fury is too
Poorly sated by killing someone, who
    think they have to gnaw
A man's breast and limbs and face for
    a kind of food. If he saw
These horrors of modern times, what
    then would Pythagoras say,
Where wouldn't he flee to escape
    them—he who abstained each day

From all live creatures as though
    they were human, and by no means
Would allow inside his belly every
    kind of bean?

XVI

the fortunate soldier·

Who, Gallius, can count the benefits
    of serving a term
In the fortunate army? If I could
    enter a camp of affirmed
Prosperity under a lucky star, I
    myself would enlist
As a trembling recruit. For an hour
    of generous fate will assist
You more than a letter of recommendation
    to Mars from the hands
Of Venus, or his mother, who delights
    in the Samian sands.

[7]   Let's first consider advantages all our
    soldiers now share.
Not the least of these is this, that
    no civilian would dare
To beat you up. If *he* gets beaten,
    he'd better not breathe
A word or run to the praetor, showing
    his knocked-out teeth,
His swollen face, black and blue, and
    the one eye left, so mangled
The doctor despairs of saving it.
    If he'd sue, he's entangled
With rough courts martial, a judge in
    hobnailed infantry boots

And a jury of brawny legs called up
    to hear the dispute
At the solemn bench, according to
    old army rules and the law
Of Camillus, forbidding that any
    soldier should be brought
To court outside the camp and away
    from his battle corps.
"Quite proper and just," you say,
    "that the army take on the chore
Of sentencing soldiers. If just
    complaints are deposed in my suit,
I won't miss my revenge." But the
    whole battalion will be in cahoots
Against you, each squad to a man will
    agree to give you a cure
That will make your damages won in
    court far worse to endure
Than those you complained of. You
    have two legs, but nevertheless
You must have the brains of a jackass,
    such as are possessed
By that public speaker, Vagellius,
    to rouse the vindictiveness
Of all those boots, those thousand
    hobnails. Who'd go, besides,
So far from the city, be such a
    Pylades as to ride
Along with you through the camp's
    high ramparts? You'd better dry
Your tears right now, and not solicit
    friends, who will lie
And dig up excuses. "Call in your
    witnesses," says the judge;
And if any man, whoever he be, has
    the courage to budge
And say "I saw the assault," I'll
    claim he deserves the hair
And virtuous beard our ancestors wore.
    You'll find anywhere

A false witness against a civilian
    more quickly than one who attests
The truth against a soldier's honor
    and rich interests.

[35]   Now let's note some other rewards
    and perquisites of the pledge
To serve in the army. Should some
    conniving neighbor allege
That a vale or field of my forebears'
    estate is his and dig out
The sacred boundary stone at
    mid-point, to which my devout
Respects I've paid each year with a
    gift of cakes and meal;
Should a debtor refuse to repay his
    loan and claim the seal
Is faked, the signatures forged, the
    documents null and void—
I must wait for the regular session
    of court, to be annoyed
By everyone else with lawsuits on
    the docket and face
Even then a thousand tiresome
    postponements, a thousand delays.
This happens so often—the benches
    have been arranged in a row,
Smooth-tongued Caedicius is taking
    his cloak off, but Fuscus must go
To piss, and though all's ready, the
    hearing's adjourned. In the slow,
Dragging sands of the legal arena we
    spar and fight that way.
But those privileged fellows with
    buckled belts and a fine array
Of weapons get their cases scheduled
    whenever they please,
And their funds aren't erased by
    endless chains of legalities.

Moreover, only a soldier is given
    the right to make
A will while his father lives; for
    whatever a soldier may take
As pay for his army service is held
    under law not to be
Part of the estate that the father
    controls. Therefore you see
Coranus, who follows the flag and
    earns army pay, fawned upon
By decrepit old Papa, who hopes to
    be his son's heir. The son
Is promoted for duty well done and
    reaps rewards well earned
By his noble service. The general
    surely should be concerned
That his bravest soldiers should be
    the most prosperous, too,
That all be made happy with medals
    and trappings of gold, all who

What we now have of the satire ends
at this line. Scholars have conjectured
that the complete poem would have
run to some three hundred lines, on
the basis of comparisons of structure
and on the assumption that the manuscripts from which the extant copies
were made had already lost the last
quire.

GLOSSARY

This glossary relates only to my version of the satires and does not include the names of persons about whom nothing is known beyond the indications of the text. Some of these names may be cover names for actual people of Juvenal's day, but there is little evidence to support most of the parallels. Geographical names that should be clear to the reader or are listed in a dictionary, personifications (Shame, Virtue, Nature, etc.), and deities representing certain abstractions (Fortune, Honor, Chastity, etc.) are not included unless there is an occasion, in doing so, for giving information relevant to the text. In most cases the dates for kings and rulers given below refer to the terms of their rule.

ACESTES. Mythical king of Sicily (*Aeneid,* V, 61 ff.).

ACHILLES. Legendary Greek hero of the *Iliad,* son of Peleus and Thetis. His charioteer, whom Juvenal names in I, was Automedon. His great friend, killed in the Trojan War, was Patroclus. He was instructed in music and other arts by the centaur Chiron. After his death Ajax and Ulysses contended for his armor (Ovid, *Metamorphoses,* XIII, 2 ff.).

ACILIUS. M. Acilius Glabrio, a senator. His son, of the same name, was murdered by Domitian after his triumph in the arena where the emperor had ordered him to fight.

ACTIUM. The naval battle, 31 B.C., in which Cleopatra and Mark Antony were defeated by Agrippa and Octavius. In VIII Juvenal says "Leucas," which is an island many miles offshore.

ACTOR. A leader of the Auruncans, defeated by Turnus, who used his spear to fight against Aeneas (*Aeneid,* XII, 94). Juvenal quotes from Vergil in this passage.

AEACUS. One of the judges in Hades. His grandson was Achilles.

AEMILIAN BRIDGE. A bridge over the Tiber built by Aemilius Scaurus.

AENEAS. Son of Venus and Anchises, who after the fall of Troy settled in Latium; hero of Vergil's *Aeneid.*

AEOLUS. God of the winds, who kept them in bags of skin or in caves of the Aeolian (Lipari) islands. (*Aeneid* I, 52 ff.)

AFRICA. Specifically, the Roman province of Africa, though other countries making up the then known continent might be included in the thought of a particular passage. Africa was the main source of grain for Rome; and, with Gaul, was notable for its orators, lawyers, and interest in eloquence.

AFRICAN KING. In V Juvenal names Bocchar, a king of Mauretania during the Second Punic War.

AGAMEMNON. Father of Orestes and one of the Greek heroes before Troy. His wife, Clytemnestra, took a lover in his absence at the war and Orestes killed both his own mother and her lover to avenge his father's honor.

AGANIPPE. A spring on Mount Helicon in Boeotia, sacred to the Muses.

AGATHYRSIANS. A Scythian people who lived on the Maris River and were tattooed blue.

AGAVE. A play by Statius.

AGRIPPA. Agrippa II, of the Herod family of Judea.

AGRIPPINA. Wife of the Emperor Claudius, who poisoned him with mushrooms. See Satire V, 147.

AJAX. Son of Telamon, king of Salamis, who committed suicide after failing in the contest with Ulysses for Achilles' armor. The passage in VII is a reference to Ovid's *Metamorphoses,* XIII. In X, "our Ajax" seems to refer to Tiberius. In XIV, Ajax in his madness slew a herd of cattle, thinking he was killing Agamemnon and Ulysses.

ALABANDA. A town in Caria near the Maeander River.

ALBA (Alban). Alba Longa, the oldest Latin town, founded by the Trojan Ascanius, son of Aeneas. It was destroyed by Tullus Hostilius, though he left unharmed the temple of Vesta and its fire, which Aeneas had brought from Troy. Domitian went to Alba each year for the Quinquatria honoring Minerva (Suetonius, *Domitian,* 4). On the omen of the white sow with a litter of thirty pigs, see *Aeneid,* III, 389–93, and VIII, 42–48.

ALCATRAZ. The U.S. prison island; Juvenal says "narrow Gyara," a small island in the Aegean Sea to which exiles were sent.

ALCESTIS. Wife of Admetus, king of Pherae in Thessaly. When the oracle said that Admetus would die unless a friend offered to die for him, she offered herself.

ALCINOUS. King of the Phaecians, a mythical people on the island of Scheria.

ALCITHOË, TEREUS, THEBES. In VII, names of unknown literary works.

ALECTO. One of the Furies.

ALEXANDER. Alexander the Great, king of Macedonia (356–323 B.C.), conqueror of the Greek city-states and the Persian Empire from Egypt and Asia Minor to India. He died at Babylon, whose city walls were famous for being made of bricks.

ALLOBROGICUS. Surname of Q. Fabius Maximus, consul in 121 B.C., who conquered the Allobroges, a Gallic people.

ALPS. A high mountain system in southwest Europe. Hannibal's army blasted the cliffs by pouring vinegar into cracks so that it would freeze overnight, with a resulting explosion of the rocks (Livy, XXI, 37).

AMMON. A Libyan god, whose temple and oracle were in the oasis of Siwa. He was worshiped by the Romans as Jupiter Ammon.

AMPHION. King of Thebes and husband of Niobe.

AMYDON. A city in Macedonia.

ANCHEMOLUS. A warrior slain by Pallas (*Aeneid*, X, 389). The scholiasts say his stepmother was Caspiria.

ANCHISES. Father of Aeneas. The name of his nurse is not known, but the nurse of Aeneas was Caieta. A secondary effect of this passage is similar to that of the gossipy woman in VI who doesn't know by name a mountain from a river.

ANCONA. A town near the middle coast of the Adriatic in Italy, founded by Greeks, 392 B.C.

ANCUS. Ancus Martius (640–616 B.C.), the fourth king of Rome.

ANDROMACHE. Wife of Hector, described as tall and of heroic proportions.

ANDROS. An island of the Cyclades in the Aegean.

ANTAEUS. A giant, son of Poseidon and Gea (goddess of earth), who could not be overcome so long as he could touch the earth. Hercules lifted him up above the ground with one hand and dashed out his brains with the other.

ANTIGONE. Daughter of Oedipus and a subject of dramas. The reference in VIII is to the role of this princess in a play.

ANTILOCHUS. Son of Nestor. He was killed by Memnon while defending his father at the siege of Troy.

ANTIOCHUS. A Greek actor. In this passage Juvenal also lists Stratocles, Demetrius, and "delicate Haemus."

ANTIPHATES. King of the Laestrygones, who were cannibals (*Odyssey*, X, 81–132).

ANTONIUS. C. Antonius, uncle of Mark Antony, was

247

expelled from the Senate for extortion, 70 B.C.

ANTONY. Marcus Antonius (Mark Antony), c. 83–30 B.C., Roman general, friend of Caesar, lover of Cleopatra. He was one of the second triumvirate with Octavius and Lepidus. Angered by the Philippics of Cicero against him, he had the orator put to death and exhibited the head and hands of the dead man on the rostra in the forum.

ANUBIS. Egyptian god, conductor of the dead to the other world.

APICIUS. M. Gabius Apicius, a famous epicure of the time of Tiberius and Augustus, who wrote a cook book that has come down to the present, though in degenerate form. There were two other gluttons named Apicius.

APOLLO. Son of Jupiter and Latona, brother of Diana. He was god of music, poetry, prophecy, and the sun. In VI the "goddess" in line 172 is Diana.

APOLLO'S COURT. In the Forum of Augustus was a statue of Apollo, where lawsuits were tried, near Apollo's temple and a library of law books.

APPIAN. Of an old noble family; related to Appius Claudius.

APPIAN WAY. The oldest Roman road, built in 312 B.C. by the censor Appius Claudius. It ran from Rome to Capua (near Naples) and later was extended to Brundisium.

APULIA. A region in southern Italy.

AQUINUM. A town in Latium, birthplace of Juvenal. A temple to Diana and one to Ceres were located there.

ARABIA. A country in Asia. In XI, Juvenal, perhaps misled by the origins of ivory traders, was mistaken in suggesting that elephants lived in Arabia.

ARACHNE. A girl of Lydia who, forced to yield a spinning contest to Minerva, hanged herself and was changed by the goddess into a spider (Ovid, *Metamorphoses*, VI, 5 ff.).

ARCADIAN. Of a region of the Peloponnesus.

ARCTIC SEA. Juvenal says "frozen ocean."

ARICIAN HILL. Aricia was a hill town on the Appian Way near Rome.

ARISTOTLE. Greek philosopher (384–322 B.C.), a pupil of Plato and the tutor of Alexander.

ARMENIA. A country in Asia. In A.D. 115 a great comet was the omen of the fall of its king.

ARPINUM. Birthplace of Cicero (106 B.C.), who suppressed the conspiracy of Catiline in 63 B.C. The "other man" from Arpinum, following this passage, is C. Marius.

ARTAXATA. Capital of Armenia.

ARVIRAGUS. A British prince; he appears in Shakespeare's *Cymbeline*.

ASIAN KNIGHTS. In VII, the reference is to the fact that Oriental slaves often accumulated enough money (400,000 sesterces) to become knights.

ASSARACUS. Son of Tros, king of Troy and kinsman of Priam.

ASTREA. Goddess of justice, daughter of Zeus and Themis. She was the last of the deities to leave the earth (in the Iron Age, following the Silver Age) and was placed among the stars as Virgo.

ASWAN. A town on the Nile in Egypt. Juvenal calls it Syene, which was a customs station on the Roman frontier.

ATELLANE. From Atella, an ancient city of Campania. The Atellane farce was a type that was very popular in Rome.

ATHOS. A mountain at the end of the peninsula of Chalcidice in northeastern Greece. The references in this passage are to Xerxes, king of Persia, who had a canal cut across the isthmus and who crossed the Hellespont on a pontoon bridge. The "Greek histories" are probably those of Herodotus, who recounts these exploits of Xerxes.

ATLAS. Mythical king of Mauretania, of giant size, who was changed into Mount Atlas, on which the sky was supposed to rest.

ATREUS. Father of Agamemnon and Menelaus. "Son of Atreus" as an epithet for Domitian in IV is, of course, derisive. In VII, *Atreus* is the title of a drama.

ATRIDES. Son of Atreus. In VI, it means Agamemnon, as a symbol of the husband who lives in fear of being murdered by his wife.

AUGUSTUS. The name granted to Octavius when he became emperor in 27 B.C. It was later applied to all subsequent Roman emperors.

AURUNCA. A town in Campania, birthplace of Lucilius whom Juvenal calls "great nursling of Aurunca" in I.

AUTONOË. Daughter of Cadmus, mother of Actaeon. With her sisters Agave and Ino, she tore Pentheus to pieces in a frenzy, which may be the allusion in VI.

AVENTINE HILL. One of the Seven Hills of Rome.

AZOV, SEA OF. A sea northeast of the Black Sea, to which it connects. The Romans called it Lake Maeotis.

BABYLON. The chief city of Babylonia, on the Euphrates. Its walls were celebrated for being made of bricks rather than stones.

BACCHANTES. Votaries of Bacchus, god of wine; proverbial figures of revelry.

BAIAE. A favorite resort of the Romans on the coast of Campania near Naples.

BAPTAE. Worshipers of the goddess Cotytto.

BAREA. Barea Soranus, proconsul of Asia, executed by Nero (Tacitus, *Annals,* XVI, 21, 23, 33).

BATAVIANS. Inhabitants of Batavia (now Holland).

BATHYLLUS. An actor of women's roles (Tacitus, *Annals,* I, 54).

BEBRIACUM. The battle in which Vitellius' forces defeated Otho, A.D. 69.

BELLEROPHON. Son of Glaucus of Corinth. He was loved by Stheneboea, wife of Protues, king of Argos. When he scorned her love, she slandered him to her husband.

BELLONA. Usually the goddess of war, sister of Mars; but in Juvenal she is clearly the other Bellona, a goddess of Cappadocian origin whose priests behaved like those of Cybele, with self-mutilation, noisy music, and prophesying.

BELUS. Mythical founder of Babylon. His granddaughters, the Danaides (daughters of Danaus), numbered fifty and all except one murdered their husbands (the fifty sons of Aegyptus) on their wedding night.

BERENICE. Wife of her uncle Herod, king of Chalcis. She lived, after his death (A.D. 48), with her brother Agrippa II. See Acts, 23.

BITHYNIA. A country in northwest Asia Minor.

BITHYNIAN HIGHNESS. Prusias I of Bithynia.

BOÖTES. The constellation known as "the ox driver."

BOSPORUS. The straits between Thrace and Asia Minor. The "clashing rocks" are the two Cyaneae (as Juvenal calls them) at the mouth of the straits. The "skins full of storms" following this reference are those of Aeolus, keeper of the winds.

BRIGANTES. A powerful British tribe that held most of Britain north of the Humber River.

BRITANNICUS. Son of Claudius and Messalina, born A.D. 41 and killed by Nero in 55.

BRITTONES. A warlike Germanic tribe.

BRUTI. Marcus Junius Brutus (nephew of Cato the Younger) and Decimus Junius Brutus, who conspired in the murder of Julius Caesar.

BRUTIDIUS. Brutidius Niger, a public officer involved in the fall of Sejanus (Tacitus, *Annals,* III, 66).

BRUTUS. Lucius Junius Brutus, who saved his life in the reign of Tarquin the Proud (died c. 510 B.C.) by pretending to be mad. He later took the cognomen Brutus (senseless). In VIII, the reference is simply to one of such a great family.

CACUS. Son of Vulcan. He was a giant and a cattle thief and was killed by Hercules when he tried to steal the oxen of Geryon (*Aeneid,* VIII, 193 ff.).

CAESAR. In VI, concerning the scrolls against Cato, Julius Caesar, who wrote them to denigrate Cato the Elder. The reference is to Clodius, who in female disguise attended the rites of the Good Goddess in Caesar's house, 62 B.C. Caesar, at the beginning of VII, is thought by many to be Hadrian.

CAESONIA. Wife of the Emperor Caligula, who is said to have driven him mad with an infusion of *hippomanes* (Suetonius, *Caligula,* 50).

CALLIOPE. The muse of epic poetry. Juvenal's invocation of her in IV announces his parody of epic.

CALPE. One of the Pillars of Hercules, now Gibraltar.

CAMERINUS (Camerini). A man (or men) of Cameria, a town in Latium. In VIII, since the application of Camerinus is derisive, perhaps it suggests "conqueror of Cameria."

CAMILLUS. M. Furius Camillus (died 365 B.C.) was one of the heroes of the republic. Having conquered Veii and freed Rome from the Gauls, he was made dictator five times.

CAMPANIA. A district of central Italy.

CANNAE. The small town in Apulia where Hannibal defeated the Romans (216 B.C.) and slaughtered some 40,000 of their finest men.

CANOPUS. A city on the delta of the Nile famed for its depravity.

CANUSIAN. Of the town Canusium, in Apulia, which was famous for its wool.

CAPITO. Cossutianus Capito, condemned for extortion of his province, Cilicia, A.D. 58 (Tacitus, *Annals,* XIII, 33).

CAPITOL. The temple of Jupiter on the Tarpeian Rock in Rome.

CAPITOLINE. One of the Seven Hills of Rome. In VI, the games in honor of Jupiter Capitolinus, instituted by Domitian to be observed every fifth year.

CAPPADOCIA. A district of Asia Minor, north of Cilicia.

CAPRI. A small island off the coast of Campania where Tiberius spent his last ten years and from which he sent his letter to the Senate concerning Sejanus.

CARPATHIAN SEA. The waters between Rhodes and Egypt, so called from the island Carpathus (now Scarpanto).

CARTHAGE. A city in North Africa destroyed by the Romans in 146 B.C.

CARUS. Carus Metius, a notorious informer under Domitian (Tacitus, *Agricola,* 45). In this passage of I, Juvenal names the actor and his wife: Latinus and Thymele.

CASSANDRA. Daughter of Priam, given the power of prophecy by Apollo.

CASSIUS. C. Cassius Longinus, one of the conspirators against and murderers of Julius Caesar.

CASTOR. Son of Tyndarus and Leda and twin brother of Pollux. In XIV the allusion is to the use of Castor's temple as a depository for private funds, since the usual one, that of Mars, had been robbed.

CATANIAN. From Catana, near Mount Aetna.

CATILINE. L. Sergius Catilina, Roman noble who with Cethegus headed a conspiracy against the state in 63 B.C., which was discovered by Cicero. He died in battle, 62 B.C.

CATO. M. Porcius Cato (234–149 B.C.), who was a censor famed for his austerity and stern discipline; and M. Porcius Cato Uticensis (95–46 B.C.), who was a Stoic.

CATULLUS. In IV, Catullus Messalinus, an informer under Domitian; in VIII and XIII, a playwright; in XII, an unknown friend of Juvenal who was a merchant.

CATULUS. C. Lutatius Catulus, of this illustrious family, was consul in 242 B.C. and ended the First Punic War with his victory at the Aegates islands. The man in III is unknown.

CECROPID (Cecropidae). One (or more) of the de-

scendants of Cecrops, mythical first king of
Athens.

CENSOR. Originally a Roman official appointed every
four or five years to draw up the "census"—
names of citizens and assessment of their property. In later times the censors were given powers
to supervise conduct of all sorts. The office had
disappeared by the time of the empire.

CENTAUR. An imaginary monster of Thessaly, half
man and half horse.

CERES. Goddess of agriculture. It is uncertain why
she is called "Helvine" in III, unless it be that her
temple was special to a family in Aquinum known
as the Helvii or Elvii. Her temple in Rome was apparently a meeting place for men and women with
adultery in mind. Her son-in-law was Pluto, god
of the underworld, who had married her daughter,
Proserpina.

CETHEGUS. C. Cornelius Cethegus, coconspirator
with Catiline in 63 B.C. He was put to death by
Cicero in that year.

CHALDEANS. A people of Assyria, famous as astron-
omers and astrologers.

CHARON. The ferryman who took souls over the
river Styx to the underworld. The fare for the
crossing was a coin.

CHARYBDIS. A dangerous whirlpool in the straits of
Messina, opposite the rock Scylla.

CHIEF PONTIFF. In IV, Domitian.

CHIRON. Son of Saturn and Philyra. He was the centaur who taught Achilles, as well as Aesculapius
and Jason.

CHRYSIPPUS. A philosopher (280–207 B.C.) of the
Stoic school, pupil of Cleanthes.

CHRYSOGONUS. A famous singer. In the sentence in
VI, the phrase "open the vent" is a makeshift rendering of the real situation, which concerns re-
moving a ring (fibula) set into the prepuce of
singers to prevent intercourse, which was thought
detrimental to the voice. This singer is also men-

tioned in VII, along with Pollio, as a teacher of music.

CICERO. M. Tullius Cicero, statesman, author, and orator (106–43 B.C.), born at Arpinum and murdered by order of Antony. He discovered the Catilinarian conspiracy and stamped it out. After his death, his head and hands were cut off and presented to Antony. The line of his poetry quoted in X is a famous example of bad verse. Perhaps the best rendering, in terms of Roman aesthetics, is that of G. G. Ramsay in the Loeb Classical Library: "O happy Fate for the Roman State/Was the date of my great Consulate."

CILICIA (Cilician). A region in Asia Minor whose people were notorious as pirates.

CIMBRI. The Cimbrians, a Germanic tribe who with the Teutons invaded Italy and were defeated by C. Marius and Q. Lutatius Catulus.

CIRCE. An enchantress, daughter of the Sun and Perse, who lived on Aeaea. She changed the sailors of Ulysses into swine (*Odyssey*, X, 203 ff.).

CIRCUS. An oval course for races and games encircled by tiers of seats. The Circus Maximus held 100,000 spectators; others were the Circus Flaminius and the Circus Maritimus. A low wall on which were various ornaments, among them statues of dolphins and eggs, divided the center of the racing area, with three pillars at each end, around which the competitors raced. Under the arcades of the outer supporting arches of the seating structure, prostitutes and other merchants had stalls.

CIRRHA. A city of Phocis, near Delphi, and sacred to Apollo, who is the "seer" in XIII. In this passage, the huntress is Diana.

CLAUDIUS. The emperor (10 B.C.–A.D. 54). He died of a poison mushroom given him by his wife (also his niece), Agrippina (Tacitus, *Annals*, XII, 67; Suetonius, *Claudius*, 44). In VI his wife (the third) is Valeria Messalina, whom he executed in A.D. 48.

CLEANTHES. A Greek philosopher (c.331–c.232 B.C.), pupil of Zeno (who founded the Stoic school), and his successor as leader of the school.

CLEOPATRA. (c.69–30 B.C.) Queen of Egypt, daughter of Ptolemy Auletes and mistress of Mark Antony.

CLIO. Muse of history.

CLITUMNUS. A river in Umbria famed for its white cattle, which were especially desired as sacrifices to the highest gods.

CLODIUS. Publius Clodius Pulcher, a tribune. The reference in II is to his murder by his enemy, Milo, in 52 B.C. In II and VI the reference is to his violation, in the disguise of a woman, of the all-female rites of the Good Goddess, 62 B.C.

CLUVIENUS. Unknown; this may be a cover name for some other low-grade poet of the time. See Highet, *Juvenal the Satirist*, note 5, pp. 289–94, for a discussion of cover names in the satires, relating to many of the names not listed in this glossary.

CLYTEMNESTRA. Daughter of Tyndarus and wife of Agamemnon, whom she and her lover, Aegisthus, murdered. Orestes and Electra were her children.

COLCHIS. A country on the eastern shore of the Black Sea, home of Medea. Here, in the grove of Mars (Ares), a dragon guarded the Golden Fleece.

COLLINE TOWER. A gate to Rome located near the Quirinal hill.

COMMAGENIAN. Of a province in the north of Syria.

COPTUS. A city on the Nile in Egypt.

CORCYRA (Corcyraean). An island in the Ionian Sea, now Corfu.

CORINTH. A city in Greece.

CORNELIA. Daughter of Scipio Africanus, who conquered Hannibal and Syphax; wife of Ti. Sempronius Gracchus and mother of the Gracchi.

CORUS. The northwest wind.

CORYBANTS. Priests of Cybele, who indulged in orgies.

CORYDON. A shepherd. This is a quotation from Vergil's *Eclogue*, II, 2.

COS. An island in the Aegean famous for wine and fine fabrics.

COTTA. Aurelius Cotta, an orator, consul in 75 B.C.

COTYTTO. A goddess of Thrace whose festival, marked by debaucheries, was introduced at Athens. Juvenal calls her "Cecropian Cotytto," from Cecrops, the first king of Athens.

COUNCIL OF MARS. The Areopagus at Athens. It was a capital crime to reveal the votes of the members.

CRASSI. A family in the Licinius line. M. Licinius Crassus, a triumvir, was killed at Carrhae, 53 B.C.

CREMERA. A river in Etruria where 300 members of the Fabii were slain in battle, 477 B.C.

CRETE. A large island in the Mediterranean, birthplace of Jupiter (hence the allusion to "fellow-citizens"—flagons—in XIV).

CRETICUS. Surname meaning "conqueror of Crete," as Q. Metellus Creticus, who did conquer Crete. In II, an unknown judge; in VIII, a derisive name.

CRISPINUS. A rich parvenu of Egyptian origin. The name might be rendered "Kinkyhead."

CRISPUS. Vibius Crispus (Suetonius, *Domitian*, 3; Tacitus, *Histories*, II, 10).

CROESUS. King of Lydia (560–546 B.C.), famed for his wealth.

CUMAE. An ancient city (founded c. 750 B.C.) on the coast of Campania, home of the Sibyl.

CURII. An early family of Rome famous for its temperance.

CURIUS. M. Curius Dentatus, consul in 290 and 275 B.C., conqueror of the Sabines, the Samnites, and Pyrrhus. Famous for his frugal nature.

CYBELE. Phrygian goddess identified with the Asiatic Great Mother. The worship of her rites was characterized by orgiastic actions and self-mutilation. In III Juvenal speaks of her as the "Idaean divinity" to recall Mount Ida in Phrygia.

CYCLADES. A group of small islands in the Aegean.

CYCLOPES. Members of a gigantic race of one-eyed men. The most famous was Polyphemus.

CYNIC, THE NAKED. Diogenes. See Plutarch, *Alexander,* for this incident.

CYNICS. Members of a school of philosophy deriving from Antisthenes of Athens (born c. 445 B.C.), a friend of Socrates. His teachings held that virtue was necessary for happiness and consisted of freedom from wants by avoiding pleasure and desire. Socrates was the teacher of Antisthenes.

CYNTHIA. The beloved of Propertius, who addressed his poems to her, using this cover name. In this passage of VI, the girl who wept at the sparrow's death is Catullus' Lesbia (see Catullus, *Carmina,* III).

DACIA. A country on the lower Danube whose conquest was commemorated in a coin.

DAEDALUS. A mythological Greek architect of Athens who built the Minotaur's labyrinth and fashioned wings on which he and his son, Icarus, flew from Crete. Icarus fell into the sea when the wax in his wings melted, and Daedalus landed at Cumae.

DAILY GAZETTE. This was the *acta diurna,* published daily in Rome from 59 B.C. and giving reports of political and social events.

DALMATIA. A country on the eastern side of the Adriatic.

DECII. P. Decius Mus and his son of the same name, of low origins, who pledged their lives to save their country, the former in the Latin War, 340 B.C., and the latter in the battle of Sentinum, 295 B.C.

DELPHI. A small town in Phocis, famous for its oracle of Apollo. The Delphic oracle was finally abolished by emperor Theodosius in A.D. 390.

DEMOCRITUS. The "laughing philosopher" of Abdera in north Thrace (c. 460–c. 370 B.C.). In this passage, the philosopher who wept was Heraclitus of Ephesus (fl. c. 510 B.C.).

DEMOSTHENES. Famous Athenian orator (384–322 B.C.). His father was a blacksmith, or armorer.

DERBY WINNERS. Juvenal here names two famous horses, Coryphaeus and Hirpinus.

DEUCALION. Son of Prometheus, king of Phthia in Thessaly, married to Pyrrha. On the passage in I, see Ovid, *Metamorphoses,* I, 318 ff.

DIANA. The virgin goddess of the moon and of hunting, daughter of Latona and sister of Apollo.

DIDO. Daughter of Belus of Tyre, sister of Pygmalion and queen of Carthage, who loved Aeneas and killed herself when he abandoned her (*Aeneid,* I–IV).

DIOGENES. A Greek Cynic philosopher (c. 412–323 B.C.).

DIOMEDES. Legendary Greek hero, son of Tydeus (Juvenal calls him Tydides). He was second in strength to Achilles at the siege of Troy and threw a stone bigger than two men could lift, hitting Aeneas (*Iliad,* V, 302 ff.).

DOLABELLA. Cornelius Dolabella, who was condemned for extortion in Cilicia in 78 B.C.

DOMITIUS. Not Domitian, the emperor, but an earlier, nobler member of the family, such as Cn. Domitius Ahenobarbus, consul in 122 B.C., who conquered the Allobrogians, or L. Domitius Ahenobarbus, consul in 54 B.C.

DRUSI. The family descending from Livia, whose son by Augustus was named Drusus.

DRUSUS. In III probably a reference to the emperor Claudius, whose cognomen was Drusus and who was "sleepy"; in VIII, a reference to the ancient family of Livia.

EGERIA. A water nymph who instructed Numa Pompilius (Livy, I, 19).

EGNATIUS. Publius Egnatius Celer, who accused and caused the execution of Barea Soranus (Tacitus, *Annals*, XVI, 32; *Histories*, IV, 10).

EGYPTIAN. In I, 130, Juvenal says "Arabarch" (an Egyptian magistrate), which may allude to Tiberius Julius Alexander, a Jew who was prefect of Egypt in A.D. 67–70. The point of this passage turns on the law against defiling the statues of great men.

ELECTRA. Daughter of Agamemnon and Clytemnestra, sister of Orestes.

ELPENOR. One of Ulysses' crew, who were changed into pigs by Circe (*Odyssey*, X, 552–63).

ENDSVILLE. Contemporary term for an undesirable town. Juvenal names Ulubrae.

ENDYMION. A beautiful youth loved by the moon goddess.

EPICURUS. Athenian philosopher (342–270 B.C.), founder of the Epicurean school.

ERIPHYLE. Wife of Amphiaraus, whom she persuaded, bribed by a gold necklace from Polynices, to join the war of the Seven Against Thebes, although by his powers of foresight he knew he would be killed.

ESQUILINE HILL. One of the Seven Hills of Rome, presumably cooler and more favored by the rich for homes.

ETHIOP, ETHIOPIAN. Of the region in Africa south of Egypt.

ETRUSCAN. Of Etruria, a district in northwest Italy (Tuscany).

EUGANEAN. Of Eugania, a country in northern Italy.

EUPHRANOR. Famous Greek sculptor (fl. 336 B.C.).

EUPHRATES. A river flowing through Syria and Babylon to join the Tigris. The reference in I is to the fact that so many slaves were from the Orient, where their earlobes were punctured with holes for rings.

EUROPA. Beautiful daughter of Agenor, king of the Phoenicians. Jupiter, in the form of a bull, carried her away to Crete.

EURUS. The southeast wind.

EVANDER. Son of Carmenta, from Arcadia. He founded Pallateum at the base of the Palatine Hill. On his entertainment of Hercules, see *Aeneid,* VIII, 359–65.

FABII, FABIUS. An illustrious family claiming descent from Hercules, many of whose members were historians, warriors, consuls, etc.

FABIUS. In VII, Paulus Fabius Maximus, patron of Ovid. Often, elsewhere, a prototype of degenerate nobility.

FABIUS GURGES. Son of Q. Fabius, the censor.

FABRICIUS. C. Fabricius Luscinus, consul in 282 and 278 B.C., who conquered the Samnites and fought against Pyrrhus. Censor in 275 B.C., he was noted for his severity against the increasing luxury of the Romans.

FALERNIAN WINE. A fine wine from a region in Campania.

FATES. Clotho, who spins; Lachesis, who measures; and Atropos, who cuts the thread. In IX, 135–36, Juvenal names the first two.

FIDENAE. A town near Rome.

FIELD. The Field of Mars, *Campus Martius,* adjacent to the Tiber.

FLAMINIAN WAY. A road built by C. Flaminius Nepos, leading north from Rome. In I, the Latin Road is also named.

FLAVIANS, FLAVII. Members of an old Roman family. In IV, the "last Flavian" is Domitian, whom Juvenal calls "a baldheaded Nero."

FLOOD. The story of a cataclysmic flood is not confined to the Bible. See Ovid, *Metamorphoses,* I, 253 ff.

FLORA. In II, an unknown woman. Elsewhere, the goddess of flowers and spring. The Floralian games were held from April 28–May 3 and were marked by indecent female behavior.

FONTEIUS. C. Fonteius Capito, consul in A.D. 67.

FORTUNE. Goddess of Fortune, whose temple at Praeneste was enormous.

FORUM. An open square, or marketplace. In most usages here, a center of commercial, political, and judicial affairs.

FRUSINO. A town in Latium. In III, in this passage, Juvenal also lists Fabrateria, another town.

FURY, FURIES. Avenging deities with snakes in their hair. The names of the three were Alecto, Megaera, and Tisiphone. In VI Juvenal specifies only the last one.

FUSCUS. Cornelius Fuscus, prefect of the Praetorian Guard. He was killed in Domitian's wars in Dacia (Romania), A.D. 86–88. In XII and XVI, unknown.

GABII. An ancient town near Rome.

GAETA. A seacoast town on the borders of Latium and Campania.

GAETULIA (Gaetulian). A country in northwest Africa. The Gaetulian sea would be off its coast.

GALATIA. "New Gaul," a country in Asia Minor settled by Celtic people.

GALBA. Sergius Sulpicius Galba, emperor A.D. 68–69.

GALLICUS. Rutilius Gallicus, prefect of the city under Domitian.

GALLINARIAN WOODS. A forest south of Rome, a haunt of criminals.

GAMES. All forms of sports, pageants, parades, shows, and plays, usually in honor of a deity. They were performed in the circuses, forums, amphitheaters, temples, or theaters and were a major part of the life and artistic sustenance of Romans in the first and second centuries. The drama, in fact, degenerated into mime plays (or ballets); and cruelty, combined with sexuality, seemed the order of the day. The major games were the Roman, Plebeian, Megalesian, Floralian, and Cerealian.

GANYMEDE. Son of the Trojan king Tros. His beauty was so great that Jove sent an eagle to kidnap him so he could be his cupbearer on Olympus. His statue in the temple of Peace was a place of rendezvous.

GAUL. In general, present-day France. Here, as in Africa and Spain, were great schools of eloquence for orators and lawyers. The inhabitants of Gaul wore trousers, in contrast to the togas and tunics of Romans.

GAURUS. A mountain in Campania.

GERMAN (Germany). In IV the tribes named are the Chatti and the Sycambri. In VI the reference is to coins commemorating victories over the Germans. In X the "German chariot" refers to the war trophy in which C. Marius rode at his triumph after victory over the German tribe of Teutons.

GIANTS. The giants were thought to have been born of lumps of earth. See Ovid, *Metamorphoses,* I.

GOLDEN FLEECE. The skin of a ram with fleece of gold given to Phrixus and Helle to aid their escape from a hated stepmother. Helle fell into the sea from the flying ram and Phrixus sacrificed the animal to Zeus when safe in Cholchis, giving the fleece to the king, Aeëtes, who put it in a tree with a dragon to guard it. Jason stole the fleece to return it, as a condition of his inheriting his share of the kingdom of his uncle Pelias.

GOOD GODDESS. *Bona Dea*; the name of Fauna, wife (or daughter) of Faunus, god of fertility. The celebration of her rites, which were forbidden to men, degenerated into an orgy.

GORGONS. The three daughters of Phorcus—Medusa, Stheno, and Euryale. The principal Gorgon was Medusa, who had snakes for hair and whose look turned a person to stone.

GRACCHI. Tiberius Gracchus (died 133 B.C.) and

Gaius Gracchus (died 121 B.C.), tribunes of the people, whose agitation for reforms fomented riots; both were murdered while engaged in such activities.

GRACCHUS. In II, probably a cover name; a reference to the noble Gracchi family rather than a specific person, but meant to typify the degenerate nobility. He is here shown as one of the Salii, priests of Mars.

GREAT ALTAR. The altar of Hercules, the care of which was traditionally that of the Fabian family.

GREEN SOX. A substitution (in modern baseball terms) for one of the racing factions—White, Red, Blue and Green. The emperors usually favored the Greens.

GUADALQUIVIR. A river in Spain; Juvenal says "Baetica," a province named for the Baetis river (now the Guadalquivir), which was famous for the naturally gold-colored wool of its sheep.

GYARA. An island of the Cyclades in the Aegean.

HAEMUS, CARPOPHORUS. Actors, "matinee idols."

HANNIBAL. Son of Hamilcar Barca and leader of the Carthaginians in the Second Punic War. He was defeated by Scipio Africanus at Zama (201 B.C.). Before this he had invaded Spain and Gaul, crossed the Alps, and threatened Rome. See Livy, XXVI, 10, for the passage on the Colline gate in VI. He committed suicide with a poison ring (c. 183 B.C.).

HARPY. A ravenous monster of Greek mythology, with a woman's head and a bird's body. Juvenal names one of them: Celaeno.

HEBE. Daughter of Jupiter and cupbearer of the gods.

HECTOR. Son of King Priam of Troy, bravest of the Trojans. He was killed by Achilles.

HECUBA. Wife of Priam, king of Troy.

HELVIDIUS. Helvidius Priscus, son-in-law of Thrasea, who was banished by Nero (Tacitus, *Annals,* XVI, 28–35) and executed by Vespasian (Suetonius, *Vespasian,* 15).

HERCULES. Greek mythological hero of great strength and courage, famous for his "twelve labors."

HERMES. Greek god, identified with Mercury.

HERNICAN. Relating to the Hernici, an ancient people of Latium.

HESPERIDES. Daughters of Hesperus, the evening star, who lived in the extreme west of the world and kept a garden of golden apples, the entrance to which was guarded by a dragon.

HIPPOLYTUS. Son of Theseus. He was accused by his stepmother, Phaedra, after he rejected her advances, of attacking her.

HISPO. Perhaps Eppuleius Proculus Hispo, consul in A.D. 101. See Highet, *Juvenal the Satirist,* note 5, pp. 291–92.

HOMER. Greek epic poet of the *Iliad* and the *Odyssey.*

HORACE. Quintus Horatius Flaccus (65–8 B.C.), son of a freedman of the Horatian family. He was one of Rome's greatest poets. In I Juvenal calls his predecessor in satire "the Venusian" because he was born at Venusia.

HORATIUS. Horatius Cocles, who held the Sublician bridge against Porsena's army (c. 510 B.C.). The "girl who swam" the Tiber was Cloelia, a hostage (Livy, II, 9, ff.).

HYACINTHUS. A beautiful Spartan youth, beloved of Apollo, who accidentally killed him and caused the flower bearing his name to spring from his blood.

HYLAS. A youth beloved of Hercules, drowned by the water nymphs, naiads.

HYMETTUS. A mountain near Athens, famous for honey and marble.

IARBAS. King of Gaetulia and a suitor of Dido (*Aeneid,* IV, 36). On the "jeweled sword," see *Aeneid,* IV, 261–62. In this passage the "drunk cobbler" was Vatinius of Beneventum, whose long nose probably caused these vessels with long spouts to be called Vatinian cups.

ICARUS. Greek mythological son of Daedalus, who made wings for their escape flight from Crete. Icarus flew too near the sun, and the wax of his wings melted, causing him to fall into the sea.

ICELAND. An island in the North Atlantic. Juvenal says "Thule," which may be Iceland or one of the Shetland islands.

IDA. In III, a mountain in Phrygia, near Troy, associated with Cybele; in XIII, a mountain in Crete where Jupiter grew up.

IDUMEAN GATE. A gate presumably associated with Jews and with Syrian perfumers.

ILIAD. Homer's epic of the siege of Troy.

IMPORTED MOTHER. Cybele, because her worship had been brought to Rome from Phrygia in 204 B.C.

IO. Daughter of King Inachus and the beloved of Jupiter, who changed her into a white cow, and in this shape she wandered to Egypt, where she became identified with Isis (Ovid, *Metamorphoses,* I, 588 ff.).

IONIAN SEA. The sea between Italy and Greece, named for Io, who swam across it.

IPHIGENIA. Daughter of Agamemnon, king of Mycenae, who sacrificed her to assure safety for the Greek ships sailing to Troy. In later tradition, a deer was substituted as the actual victim.

ISAEUS. A rhetorician of Assyria (not the Greek orator of the same name).

ISIS. Egyptian goddess whose worship had been brought into Rome near the end of the Republic and whose temple was the scene of lewd behavior and a meeting place for pimps and whores. The park in VI is probably the Lucullan gardens, another favorite spot for assignations. In XII the reference to Isis as a nourisher of painters is due to the fact that her temple was cluttered with votive tablets of shipwrecked sailors.

IULUS (Iulian). Ascanius, the son of Aeneas, who brought the Trojans to Latium.

JANUS. An old Italian deity, with two faces, looking forward and backward (hence, January).

JASON. Son of Aeson, king of Thessaly, who led the Argonauts to steal the Golden Fleece. A painting of the Argonauts adorned the walls of the Portico of Agrippa, but in winter the canvas stalls of the market shut out the view—thus, Jason is called "merchant" because of his picture in the market.

JERUSALEM. A chief city in Judea, which the Romans called Solyma, its ancient name. In this passage, "priestess with a tree as temple" refers to the provision that Jews should camp outside the city walls under trees.

JEWS. There had long been a large Jewish colony in Rome. Judea had been conquered by Pompey the Great years before the birth of Christ. By A.D. 19 the Jews in Rome were so numerous and troublesome that Tiberius could transport 4,000 of them to Sardinia (Tacitus, *Annals,* II, 85; Suetonius, *Tiberius,* 36). The first Christians filtered into Rome through the already established colony. Juvenal, though more than skeptical of the Roman gods, did not like the Jews and confused their religion with that of the Christianized Jews. The basket of hay was apparently used by custom for keeping already cooked food warm for the Sabbath, when no cooking (or other work) was to be done. At the time of writing III, Juvenal looked upon Jews as beggars or fortune-tellers. For a Roman's view of Jewish history, citing Moses as leader and lawgiver, see Tacitus, *Histories,* V, 1–13.

JOVE. Jupiter, famous for his adulteries in disguise. In XIV the "noble birds" are eagles, which carried his thunderbolts and did his bidding.

JULIA. Daughter of the Emperor Titus, guilty of incest with her uncle Domitian, who caused her death by abortion about A.D. 91. The "moral law" in this passage is the Julian law against adultery (see below).

JULIAN LAW. *Lex Iulia de adulteriis,* established under Augustus to punish adulterers, was revived by Domitian; *Lex Iulia de maritandis ordinibus* (referred to in VI) was meant to encourage marriage.

JUNCUS. Aemilius Juncus, consul in A.D. 127.

JUNO. Daughter of Saturn, wife and sister of Jupiter, and goddess of women. In II the point of swearing by her is that men would swear by Jupiter.

JUPITER. The supreme Roman god (corresponding to Greek Zeus), husband and brother of Juno. When he drove out his father, Saturn, the Siver Age began (Ovid, *Metamorphoses,* I, 113 ff.).

KENT. A county in England. In IV Juvenal says "Rutupiae" (Richborough), which is in Kent.

KING ROOSTER. Domitian.

KNIGHTS. *Equites,* originally a division of the Roman army but later more of a class distinction. This order of citizens ranked next below that of senators, and members were required to own at least 400,000 sesterces (equivalent to about $30,000). Their badge of position was a gold ring and a purple stripe on their mantles.

LACEDAEMONIAN. Of Lacedaemon, or Sparta.

LACHESIS. The one of the three Fates who measures the thread of life.

LAESTRYGONES. A race of giant cannibals in Sicily (*Odyssey,* X, 87–132).

LAGUS. Father of Ptolemy I, king of Egypt.

LAMIAN. Of the Lamii, a prominent family, used by Juvenal to symbolize nobility. In IV "Lamian blood" alludes to the many noble families decimated by Domitian before he was killed by a freedman.

LARES. Tutelary and household deities of the Romans.

LATERAN PALACE. The home of Plautius Lateranus, executed by Nero, A.D. 65, for joining Piso's conspiracy (Tacitus, *Annals,* XV, 60).

LATERANUS. Perhaps Plautius Lateranus, a nobleman of Nero's day, though Juvenal's portrait does not jibe with that of Tacitus except on the point of his being very big (Tacitus, *Annals,* XI, 36; XIII, 11; XV, 49, 53, 60).

LATIN WAY. One of the roads leading out of Rome.

LATIUM. The district in Italy in which Rome was situated.

LATONA. Mother of Apollo and Diana.

LAUREOLUS. A bandit who was crucified and about whom a mime play was written.

LAVINUM. A town in Latium built by Aeneas and named for his second wife, Lavinia.

LEDA. Wife of Tyndarus, who coupled with Zeus in the form of a swan, and later with her husband. The result was Pollux and Helen by Zeus, and Castor and Clytemnestra by her husband.

LENTULUS. In VI, VIII, and X, unknown; in VII, P. Lentulus Spinther, who as consul in 57 B.C. helped recall Cicero from exile.

LEPIDUS. M. Aemilius Lepidus, consul in 79 B.C.; and M. Aemilius Lepidus, triumvir with Antony and Octavius, 43 B.C.

LIBURNIANS. A people of Illyria (Yugoslavia and Albania today).

LIBYA. A region of North Africa, which sent much grain to Rome. The "gourmet" in V who addresses Libya is named Alledius by Juvenal.

LIGURIAN. Of Liguria, a country on the northwest coast of Italy.

LONGINUS. C. Cassius Longinus, a famous lawyer and consul, banished by Nero A.D. 65 (Tacitus, *Annals,* XVI, 7–9). His ancestor of the same name was one of the murderers of Julius Caesar.

LUCAN. M. Annaeus Lucanus (A.D. 39–65) from

Corduba in Spain, who wrote the *Pharsalia* and was executed by Nero.

LUCANIAN. Of Lucania, a country in southern Italy.

LUCILIUS. The first Roman satirist (c. 180–103 B.C.). In I Juvenal names him by epithet as the "great nursling of Aurunca," that town in Campania having been his birthplace.

LUCRETIA. A beautiful Roman lady whose suicide after being raped by Sextus Tarquinius in 510 B.C. led to the expulsion of the Tarquin kings and the beginning of the Republic (Livy, I, 58).

LUCRINE BAY. Near Baiae and celebrated for its oysters.

LUCUSTA. A notorious poisoner of Nero's time. See Tacitus, *Annals,* XII, 66, 67; Suetonius, *Nero,* 33.

LUPERCAN PRIESTS. These men officiated at the festival of the Lupercalia, wearing skins, and struck women with thongs made of sacrificed animals to produce fertility.

LYCIAN. Of Lycia, a country in Asia Minor.

LYCISCA. The name used by the empress Messalina when she spent nights in brothels.

LYONS. Formerly Lugdunum, in Gaul, where Caligula set up a rhetorical contest with severe penalties for the losers (Suetonius, *Caligula,* 20).

MAECENAS. Gaius Cilnius Maecenas (c. 70–8 B.C.), a statesman and rich patron of the arts, especially of Vergil and Horace.

MAENADS. Votaries of Bacchus, or in VI, the maddened votaries of Priapus.

MAMERCI. Descendants of Aemilius Mamercus, one of the first quaestors to be appointed at the start of the Republic. Tacitus often refers to Mamercus Aemilius Scaurus, senator and consul under Tiberius, and calls him aristocratic, eloquent, but dissolute.

MARCELLUS, MARCELLI. An ancient family of Rome. M. Claudius Marcellus defeated Hannibal at Nola.

MARIUS. In I and VIII, Marius Priscus, proconsul of Africa, who, though tried and exiled for extortion in his province in A.D. 100, was not forced to give up his plunder. In X, Caius Marius (157–86 B.C.), born near Arpinum, who defeated the Teutons near Vercelli in 102 B.C., while his colleague, Q. Lutatius Catulus, defeated the Cimbri in 101 B.C. Catulus shared in the triumph of Marius. Defeated in the civil war by Sulla, he hid in the Minturnan swamps, was imprisoned, but escaped and fled to Carthage.

MARS. God of war, son of Juno and Jupiter. The "grove of Mars" in I was the birthplace of his sons, Romulus and Remus. In II the "rugged plain" is the Campus Martius, the Field of Mars. For the loud voice of "Homer's Mars" in XIII, see *Iliad*, V, 859–63. In X the reference is to his being trapped in a net with Venus while making love.

MARSIAN. Relating to the Marsi, an ancient tribe of Latium.

MARSYAS. A Phrygian satyr who challenged Apollo to a musical contest. When the Muses gave the prize to Apollo, he had Marsyas bound and flayed alive (Ovid, *Metamorphoses*, VI, 382 ff.).

MASSA. Babius Massa, a dreaded informer under Domitian (Tacitus, *Agricola*, 45).

MATTERHORN. The mountain in Switzerland. Juvenal names Niphates, a mountain in Armenia, which most translators and commentators say "is meant for a river."

MEDEA. Daughter of Aeëtes, king of Colchis. She was famous for her magical arts. When she eloped with Jason and her father pursued, she cut her brother to pieces and cast him out to delay her father; when Jason wants to leave her, later, and marry the daughter of Creon, king of Corinth, she murders their two sons as well as Creon and his daughter.

MEGALESIAN GAMES. These games in honor of Cybele began on April 4, about five months after the plebeian games in November, which are named by Juvenal to define the period when there were no games to attend.

MELANIPPA. Sister of Antiope, queen of the Amazons—a role played by Nero.

MELEAGER. Son of Oeneus, king of Calydon. A great boar was sent to Calydon by Diana and was slain by Meleager.

MEMNON. The colossal statue of Memnon at Thebes in Egypt, which though broken gave out musical sounds when the rays of the sun struck it at daybreak.

MEMPHIS. An ancient city in Egypt.

MENOECEUS. Son of Creon, king of Thebes, who sacrificed his life when an oracle said this act would save his country.

MENTOR. Famous artist in metals, especially silver (fl. before 356 B.C.).

MEROË. An island in the Nile.

MESSALINA. Wife of the Emperor Claudius. In X, the handsome youth she intends to wed is Gaius Silius (Tacitus, *Annals,* XI, 12, 26 ff.).

METELLUS. In III and VI, L. Caecilius Metellus, who lost his eyesight when he saved the image of Minerva from her burning temple (241 B.C.). In XV, Q. Caecilius Metellus, who warred against Sertorius in 79–72 B.C.

MILETUS. A town in Asia Minor.

MILO. T. Annius Milo Papianus, who killed his enemy, Clodius, in 52 B.C.

MINERVA. Daughter of Jupiter, goddess of wisdom, patroness of all arts and sciences. The head of the Gorgon Medusa was set in her shield.

MINOTAUR. A monster, half bull and half man, imprisoned in a labyrinth on Crete. He was killed by Theseus.

MINTURNAE. A town in Latium, near marshes on the Liris River.

MITHRIDATES. King of Pontus (120–36 B.C.) who invented an antidote for poisons.

MOLOSSIA (Molossians). A district of Epirus, whose king was Pyrrhus.

MONYCHUS. A centaur (half man, half horse); the reference is to the battle of the centaurs and the Lapithae.

MOTHER EARTH. Juvenal says "Terra," the earth as a goddess.

MUCIUS. P. Mucius Scaevola, presumably, who was consul in 133 B.C. The quotation in I is apparently from Lucilius. In VIII the reference is to his burning off his right hand in a fire for failure to kill the right enemy of his people (Livy, 2).

MUSES. The nine daughters of Zeus and Mnemosyne, who were goddesses of poetry, song, drama, dancing, astronomy, etc.: Calliope, Clio, Erato, Euterpe, Melpomene, Polyhymnia, Terpsichore, Thalia, and Urania.

MYCENAE. A city in Argolis, whose king was Agamemnon.

MYRON. Famous Greek sculptor (c. 430 B.C.) of statues such as the *Discobolus* and *Marsyas*.

NARCISSUS. The powerful and very wealthy freedman of the Emperor Claudius. For his part in the death of Messalina, see Tacitus, *Annals*, XI, 33–37.

NEPTUNE. God of the oceans.

NERO. C. Claudius Nero, emperor (A.D. 54–68), noted for his debaucheries. On his acting, see Suetonius, *Nero*, 21, and Tacitus, Annals, XIV, 15. The "bald Nero" in IV is Domitian. The uncle of Nero in VI is Caligula. Nero killed, among many others, his wife and his sister. In VIII, 213, the punishment is that of a parricide, which was to be enclosed in a sack with a dog, an ape, a snake, and a cock and then thrown into the sea.

NESTOR. King of Pylos, oldest of the Greeks besieging Troy, and father of Antilochus.

NILE. The river in Egypt that in season flooded or dwindled. There were seven mouths in its delta.

NIOBE. Wife of Amphion, by whom she had seven sons and seven daughters. When she prided herself above Latona in bearing children, Latona's son and daughter took revenge, with Apollo slaying the sons and Diana the daughters (Ovid, *Metamorphoses,* VI, 146 ff.).

NORTIA. The Etruscan goddess of fortune and fate.

NUMA. Numa Pompilius (715–672 B.C.), second king of Rome following Romulus. He was instructed by night in civil and religious government by the nymph Egeria (Livy, I, 19).

NUMANTIA. A town in Spain, destroyed by Scipio the Younger in 134 B.C.

NUMBSKULL LAND. Juvenal says "land of muttonheads," referring to Abdera, which was reputed to be a breeding place of blockheads, but produced the philosopher Democritus.

NUMIDIA. A country in North Africa. The oil exported to Rome had an unpleasant odor.

OCTAVIUS. C. Octavianus, the Emperor Augustus (63 B.C.–A.D. 14). With Antony and Lepidus, he made up the second triumvirate and was victor in battles at Actium and Philippi.

OLYMPIAN. Of Mount Olympus, the home of the gods. The Olympian games were held in honor of Zeus at Olympia, and the winner received a wreath of wild olive.

OLYNTHUS. A town in Thrace, Chalcidice, on the borders of Macedonia.

OMBI. A town in upper Egypt.

ORESTES. In I, an imaginary tragedy based on Orestes, son of Agamemnon and Clytemnestra. He killed his mother and her lover and was tormented by the Furies for his crime. His sister was Electra, his wife Hermione, daughter of Menelaus.

ORKNEYS. Juvenal says "Orcades," which are the Orkney and Shetland islands off the north coast of Scotland, conquered during the reign of Claudius.

ORONTES. The principal river of Syria.

OSIER HEIGHTS. The Viminal Hill, which Juvenal calls "the hill named for the osier."

OSIRIS. One of the chief Egyptian gods, brother and husband of Isis. At first a nature god who died and was reborn in the spring, he later became a god of the dead and was associated with Anubis, the conductor of the dead to the other world. Osiris was thought to inhabit a bull, Apis, that was periodically sacrificed. When a new Apis was found, the people cried, "We have found him! Let us rejoice together!"

OSTIA. The harbor and port of Rome, at the mouth of the Tiber.

OTHO. M. Salvius Otho (A.D. 32–69), Roman emperor for three months, notorious in youth for his vices, often in companionship with Nero. He committed suicide after his defeat at Bebriacum. In VI the "great citizen feared by Otho" is the emperor Galba, whose death he caused. Also, in XIV, L. Roscius Otho (see Otho's law).

OTHO'S LAW. The law that L. Roscius Otho drew up giving special seats in the theater to knights— men whose wealth amounted to 400,000 sesterces or more.

PACTOLUS. A river in Lydia, said to bring down golden sands.

PALAEMON. Q. Remmius Palaemon (first century A.D.), who wrote an important work on grammar.

PARIS. A famous dancer-actor; there were two of these Parises, one a favorite of Nero, who had him executed as a rival in A.D. 67; the other a favorite of Domitian, who had him executed in A.D. 87. In X, of course, it is the legendary Paris, son of Priam, whose "rape" of Helen set off the Trojan War.

PARRHASIUS. A famous Greek painter of Ephesus, fl. c. 400 B.C.

PARTHIA. A country in Asia southeast of the Caspian Sea.

PAULUS. L. Aemilius Paulus, who was one of the commanders at the battle of Cannae, 216 B.C., and was killed there. In VII, unknown; in VIII, a branch of the ancient Aemilian family.

PEGASUS. In IV, a magistrate and member of Domitian's council. See Highet, *Juvenal the Satirist*, note 14, pp. 259–61, for a discussion of the men on Domitian's council as listed in IV. Elsewhere, Pegasus, the winged horse (associated with the Muses) that sprang from the blood of Medusa, one of the Gorgons. Juvenal speaks of him as the "Gorgonian steed." Tarsus, on the river Cydnus in Cilicia, is the place where the feather dropped from his wing.

PELEUS. King of Thessaly and father of Achilles.

PELOPEA. "Daughter of Pelops," a pantomime play in which the title role was acted by Paris.

PENELOPE. Wife of Ulysses who wove during his absence at the Trojan War.

PETOSIRIS. An ancient Egyptian astrologer.

PHAEACIAN. Relating to a mythical people of the island of Scheria, where autumn was perpetual.

PHAEDRA. Daughter of Minos, king of Crete; wife of Theseus; and stepmother of Hippolytus, whose death she caused by her slander to his father. Juvenal calls her the "Cretan lady."

PHALARIS. A tyrant of Agrigentum (c. 570–554 B.C.), in Sicily, who roasted his victims alive in a brass bull.

PHAROS. An island off Alexandria where a great lighthouse stood.

PHARSALUS, BATTLE OF. Fought near a town in Thessaly; Pompey was defeated by Caesar, 48 B.C.

PHIDIAS. A famous sculptor of Athens in the time of Pericles. His statues of Athena in the Parthenon and of Zeus at Olympia were made of ivory and gold.

PHILIP OF MACEDON. In 348 B.C. he arranged to bribe Lasthenes, the governor of Olynthus, a town in Chalcidice, so as to betray it into his hands.

PHILIPPI, BATTLE OF. Octavius and Antony defeated Brutus and Cassius in this battle in Macedonia, 42 B.C. Juvenal says "Thessaly," which would indicate the battle of Pharsalus, 48 B.C.; it seems that Roman poets confounded the two battles.

PHILIPPIC. In X, the second of fourteen attacks by Cicero on Mark Antony, for which reason, among others, Antony had the orator put to death.

PHILOMELA. A pantomime play, based on the sister of Procne, in which Paris played the title role.

PHOEBUS' SPOT. No reference to Phoebus Apollo. The Phoebus in VII apparently ran a bathhouse of some sort.

PHOLUS. One of the centaurs, who were famed for their drinking capacity.

PHRYGIA (Phrygian). A country in Asia Minor. In II the reference is to the self-castration of the priests of Cybele, the Phrygian goddess.

PICENUM. A district in central Italy on the Adriatic, in which Ancona was situated; it was famous for its apples.

PICUS. A mythical Latin king who was the son of Saturn and father of Faunus.

PIERIAN CAVE. A place sacred to the Muses, who are called Pierian maidens.

PISO. C. Calpurnius Piso, one of the leaders of the conspiracy against Nero, A.D. 65 (Tacitus, *Annals*, XV, 48 and elsewhere).

PITTACUS. One of the Seven Sages of Greece (seventh century B.C.).

PLUTO. King of the underworld, whose wife was Proserpina (daughter of Ceres) of Sicily. In XIII, the wheel, the rock, the vultures, are the punishments inflicted on Ixion, Sisyphus, and Tityus in the underworld.

PODUNK. Humorous name for any insignificant village. Juvenal names Fidenae and Gabii.

POLLIO. A well-known harp player. In XI, unknown.

POLYCLITUS. A famous Greek sculptor, fl. 452–405 B.C.

POLYPHEMUS. One of the Cyclopes, giants of Sicily who had only one eye. Ulysses blinded Polyphemus in order to escape from him (*Odyssey*, IX, 166 ff.).

POLYXENA. Daughter of Priam and Hecuba of Troy.

POMPEII. The family of Pompeius. In X, Pompey the Great (106–48 B.C.), triumvir with Caesar and Crassus, conqueror of Mithridates, and defeated by Caesar (Julius) at Pharsalus; and his son, Sextus Pompeius Magnus, defeated at sea by Augustus.

POMPEIUS. An informer for Domitian.

POMPEY. Gnaeus Pompey, the Great. In 50 B.C. he was seriously ill in Naples. Two years later he was murdered at Alexandria.

PONTIA. Wife of Drymis, who poisoned her husband and two children. (See Martial, VI, 75.)

PONTINE SWAMPS. A marshy region on the Appian Way.

PONTUS, KING OF. Mithridates (120–63 B.C.), who invented an antidote for poisons. He had been conquered by Sulla, Lucullus, and Pompey.

POPPAEAN CREAMS. Cosmetics named after Poppaea, wife of Nero.

POSEIDON. The Greek god of the seas (corresponding to Roman Neptune). In very early times he was perhaps more powerful than Zeus. The epithet "earthshaking" (or earthshaker) is from Homer.

POSIDES. A favorite freedman of Claudius (Suetonius, *Claudius*, 28).

PRAENESTE. A town in the mountains near Rome.

PRAETOR. A magistrate of Rome, an officer.

PRIAM. The last king of Troy, slain at a great age by Pyrrhus in the siege of Troy.

PRIAPUS. God of gardens, vineyards, and fertility. He was represented either as a phallus or as a herm with a phallus.

PROCNE. Daughter of King Pandion of Athens, who in revenge for the infidelity of her husband, Tereus, served him a dinner of his son, Itys.

PROCULEIUS. In I, unknown. In VII, a Roman knight with generous instincts (Horace, *Odes*, II, ii).

PROMETHEUS. Father of Deucalion. He stole fire from heaven and used it in making man from clay. One of the Titans, he was called "the Titan" in XIV by Juvenal.

PUNIC. Carthaginian. There were three Punic Wars, 264–241, 218–201, and 149–146 B.C.

PYGMY. A race of dwarfs living in Africa. On their battles with cranes, see *Iliad*, III, 3–6.

PYLADES. The faithful friend of Orestes.

PYLOS, KING OF. Nestor. In X the reference is to *Iliad*, I, 247–252. The comparison with the crow comes from the belief that the crow lived many times longer than man.

PYRRHA. Wife of Deucalion and daughter of Epimetheus. With her husband she regenerated human life after the flood.

PYRRHUS. King of Epirus (c. 318–272 B.C.) and as such ruler of the Molossi.

PYTHAGORAS. A Greek philosopher of Samos (c. 540 B.C.) who settled in southern Italy and founded the school named after him. Probably as a result of his journey to India, he believed in the transmigration of souls and would eat no flesh, but only vegetables.

PYTHIAN. Relating to Pytho, the old name for Delphi, and to Apollo, god of prophecy. He had killed the Python, a huge snake, near Delphi.

QUACK, DR. Juvenal names Philippus, an unknown, inferior doctor.

QUINTILIAN. M. Fabius Quintilianus (A.D. 40–100), a great rhetorician and a rich man.

QUIRINAL. Quirinus was the name given Romulus at his apotheosis. The Quirinal Hill is one of the seven in Rome.

QUIRINI. Romulus and Remus.

QUIRINUS. The name of Romulus at his apotheosis. In this passage in VIII the "last of our good kings" is Servius Tullius, born of a slave, Ocrisia, who was, says Livy, a princess before her capture; the "sons of the consul" are Titus and Tiberius, sons of L. Junius Brutus; the "tyrants," Tarquin the Proud and his party; "a slave," Vindicius (Livy, I, 58).

REEVES, STEVE. Juvenal names Corbulo, a general under Claudius and Nero who had unusual strength.

REMUS. Twin brother of Romulus, who killed him in a quarrel at the founding of Rome (Livy, I, 3 ff.). "Remus' spawn" is the Roman people; Juvenal says "the mob of Remus."

RHADAMANTHUS. Son of Jupiter and a judge in the underworld.

ROME. The capital of Latium and the Roman Empire, founded April 21, 753 B.C., according to legend, by descendants of the Trojans, who had come with Aeneas after the fall of Troy and settled at Alba. Its population in Juvenal's time was about half a million people. Where I have used such terms as "midtown Rome" or "the heart of Rome," Juvenal has generally used *Subura,* the name of the noisiest and busiest section of the city.

ROMULUS. Son of Mars and Rhea Silvia, twin of Remus, and founder of Rome. In II Juvenal calls him "Father of our city." Because Rhea Silvia was a Vestal Virgin, her father, Numitor, ordered the babies drowned, but the basket holding them was washed aground and a she-wolf nursed them. In XI Juvenal calls the wolf "the Romulean beast." (Livy, I, 3 ff.)

ROSTRUM. The speaker's platform, or tribune, in the forum.

RUBELLIUS BLANDUS. C. Rubellius Blandus or C. Rubellius Plautus, members of a good family connected by marriage with the Julian line (Tacitus, *Annals*, XIII, 19–22; XIV, 22, 57–59; XVI, 10, 30).

RUBRIUS. Unknown, perhaps a cover name. The allusion in "satire-writing pervert" is to Nero's satire on Quintinianus (Tacitus, *Annals*, XV, 49).

RUTULIAN. Of the Rutuli, an ancient people of Latium, whose king was Turnus. In XII the reference is to the herd of elephants that the emperors kept near Laurentum.

SABBATH. The Jewish Sabbath, the seventh day of the week, Saturday, which, like the Christian Sabbath (Sunday), was a day of rest and religious observance. The Romans observed no such interruption of daily affairs. (See Tacitus, *Histories*, V, 4.)

SABINE. Referring to one of the ancient peoples of Italy, famous for sober morals and chastity. The war caused by the rape of the Sabine women was ended by all the women going into mourning and disheveling their hair (Livy, I, 13).

SAGUNTUM. A town in Spain (Juvenal calls it Zacynthos) that was loyal to Rome and was captured by Hannibal in 218 B.C. (Livy, XXI, 5–15).

SALAMIS. Great naval battle in which the Greeks defeated Xerxes and the Persians, 480 B.C.

SAMOS. An island off the coast of Asia Minor, famous for its earthenware. It was a center for worship of Juno, as indicated in XVI.

SAMOTHRACE. An island in the north Aegean famous for mystic rites of the Cabiri.

SARDANAPALUS. Ashurbanipal (c. 668–c. 626 B.C.), king of Assyria devoted to luxury.

SATURN. A mythical king of Latium, god of agriculture and civilization (identified with the Greek Kronos) and the father of Jupiter. His reign was the Golden Age. He was driven from power by his son, Jupiter, whose reign was the Silver Age. As a planet, Saturn was unlucky.

SCANTINIAN LAW. A law against sexual perversions.

SCAURI, SCAURUS. A famous family. M. Aemilius Scaurus was censor in 109 B.C.

SCIPIO. P. Cornelius Scipio Africanus the Elder (236–164 B.C.), who conquered Hannibal; and Scipio Africanus the Younger (c. 185–129 B.C.), son of L. Aemilius Paulus and the destroyer of Carthage. The elder Scipio received the idol of Cybele when it was brought from Phrygia in 204 B.C.

SCYLLA. A rock in the Straits of Messina, opposite Charybdis.

SCYTHIANS. A general name for all nomadic tribes north of the Black and the Caspian seas.

SECUNDUS CARRINAS. An Athenian rhetorician who taught in Rome and was banished by Caligula. In the passage in VII, the man whom Athens "saw low in poverty" was of course Socrates.

SEJANUS. L. Aelius Sejanus, son of Seius Strabo and a favorite of Tiberius. In the absence of the emperor, Sejanus, as praetorian prefect, assumed more and more power, but a letter that Tiberius sent from Capri, A.D. 29, advised the Senate to take action. Sejanus was executed, and his body was thrown into the Tiber. (See Tacitus, *Annals,* for the early actions of Sejanus; the account of his death would be in the lost books of the *Annals.*) Sejanus was a native of Volsinii, an Etruscan (Tuscan) town.

SEMIRAMIS. Wife of Ninus, king of Assyria, who after his death ruled and led the armies.

SENATOR. One of the highest positions in Rome. Augustus limited the Senate to 600 members who must have minimum property qualifications of a million sesterces. In I, 108–09, Juvenal names a senator, Corvinus, and two rich freedmen, Pallas and Licinus.

SENECA. L. Annaeus Seneca (5 B.C.–A.D. 65), who was a Stoic philosopher and writer, tutor of Nero, and a rich man who gave generously to his poorer friends. He committed suicide by opening his veins, on Nero's order (Tacitus, *Annals,* XV, 60–63).

SENONES. The Gauls who defeated the Romans in the battle of Allia, 390 B.C.

SERBIAN. Juvenal says "Moesian," referring to a tribe between Thrace and the Danube.

SERIPHOS. An island of the Cyclades in the Aegean, a favorite spot of exile.

SERVIAN RAMPARTS. The great defense work built by Servius Tullius.

SERVIUS TULLIUS. The sixth king of Rome (578–534 B.C.).

SETIA (Setine). A town in Campania whose wine was excellent.

SEVEN HILLS. The Aventine, Caelian, Capitoline, Esquiline, Palatine, Quirinal, and Viminal hills, on and around which Rome was built.

SIBERIA. Juvenal says "Sarmatia," which is actually the south of Russia.

SIBYL. In III, the Cumaean Sibyl, or priestess, of Apollo, who gave prophecies; in VIII, possibly the Sibyl who wrote the Sibylline Books, kept in the Capitol and consulted in time of danger.

SICILIAN STRAITS. The straits of Messina between Sicily and Italy, which were only 2½ miles wide and always rough, but especially so when the south wind blew. The whirlpool of Charybdis and the rock of Scylla were in the straits.

SICILIAN TYRANTS. An allusion to Phalaris, tyrant of Agrigentum, notorious for his cruelty (see VIII, 81).

SICYON. A city in northeastern Peloponnesus.

SILANUS. Unidentified, though Tacitus includes a number of members of a prominent family under the name of Junius Silanus.

SILVANUS. The Latin god of the woods; women were not allowed to attend his rites.

SIRENS. Nymphs living on the coast of southern Italy, near Sicily, whose singing lured sailors to destruction.

SOCIAL WARS. The wars waged between 91 and

88 B.C., which gained the Roman franchise for the people of Italy.

SOCRATES (Socratic). Athenian philosopher (c. 469 –399 B.C.). Accused of undermining religion and corrupting youth, he was ordered to end his life with a cup of hemlock.

SOLON. An Athenian legislator, one of the Seven Sages of Greece (c. 639–c. 560 B.C.).

SOPHOCLES. Greek tragic poet (c. 496–406 B.C.).

SORA. A town in Latium on the Liris River.

SOUTH WIND. *Auster*, one of the winds, usually bringing rain. It was controlled by Aeolus and imprisoned in his cliff at times.

SPANISH FLY. Cantharides, a powerful aphrodisiac made from powdered Spanish flies (*Lytta vesicatoria*). Juvenal names "eruca," which was rocket salad (*Eruca sativa*; Fr. *roquette*) or any of the coleworts such as kale, rape, mustard, etc. It was thought to have powers of sexual stimulation and invigoration. Ovid, in *Remedia amoris*, 1. 799, mentions *erucas salaces*—lust-stirring rockets.

SPARTAN. Of Sparta, capital of Laconia, now in Greece.

STATIUS. P. Pampinius Statius (c. A.D. 45–96), author of *Silvae*, *Thebais*, and other works.

STENTOR. A Greek herald with a loud voice (*Iliad*, V, 785–86).

STHENEBOEA. Wife of Proetus of Argos, who slandered Bellerophon when he rejected her love and moved her husband to plot his death.

STOICS. Followers of the philosophy of Zeno, which called for a severe morality, bordering at times on asceticism.

STYX (Stygian). The river Styx in the underworld across which souls of the dead were carried by Charon, the ferryman. The dead must have in their mouths a coin to pay their passage.

SULLA. L. Cornelius Sulla (138–78 B.C.), general and dictator. The reference in I is to a favorite topic for student oratory, as to whether he should have retired from public affairs in 79 B.C. His proscriptions were continued by the second triumvirate of Antony, Octavius, and Lepidus.

SULMO. A town in the Sabine region.

SYBARIS. A town in Lucania, famous for luxury (hence, *sybarite*).

SYPHAX. King of Numidia during the Second Punic War, defeated by Scipio Africanus the Elder, who was Cornelia's father.

TAGUS. A river in Portugal and Spain whose sands were supposed to be filled with gold.

TARENTUM. A wealthy town on the coast of Magna Graecia.

TATIUS. King of the Sabines, later coregent with Romulus.

TAURIC. Of the Taurians, Scythian people on the Sea of Azov in Crimea.

TELAMON. Father of Ajax. He helped his brother Peleus murder their half brother, Phocus.

TELEPHUS. An imaginary tragedy based on Telephus, king of Mysia.

TENTYRA. A town in Egypt, now called Dendyra, or Dendra.

TEUTONS (Teutonic). A German tribe.

THABRACA. A town in Numidia.

THAÏS. A female role in a play, the prototype of a courtesan. In the passage in VI, Juvenal calls the man *Triphallus* (man with three phalli).

THALES. A philosopher of Miletus, c. 636–546 B.C.

THEBAIS. An epic by Statius in twelve books.

THEBES (in Egypt). An ancient city in upper Egypt, famous for its hundred gates.

THEBES (in Greece). A city in Boeotia, founded by Cadmus. It had seven gates.

THEODORUS. A rhetorician from Rhodes who taught at Rome.

THERSITES. One of the Greeks before Troy, noted for ugliness and a scurrilous tongue (*Iliad,* II, 212 ff.).

THESEID. An imaginary epic based on Theseus.

THESSALY. A region in the north of Greece, famous for magic potions. In VIII, referring to Octavius' triumphs, Juvenal means the battle of Philippi, often confused with the battle of Pharsalus, fought in Thessaly.

THRACE (Thracian). A region in the eastern part of the Balkan peninsula, between the Black Sea and the Aegean Sea.

THRASEA. P. Paetus Thrasea, put to death by Nero for defense of his freedom. Helvidius Priscus was his son-in-law. (Tacitus, *Annals*, XVI, 21–35.)

THRASYLLUS. The astrologer of the Emperor Tiberius (Tacitus, *Annals*, VI, 20, 21; Suetonius, *Tiberius*, 14).

THRASYMACHUS. A rhetorician, born in Carthage but practicing at Athens, who hanged himself.

THYESTES. Son of Pelops, brother of Atreus. In VIII, a role in a drama.

TIGELLINUS. Gaius Ofonius Tigellinus, a favorite of Nero (Tacitus, *Annals*, XIV–XVI). For the burning of men at the stake—a method of killing Christians—see Tacitus, *Annals*, XV, 44.

TIRESIAS. A blind soothsayer of Thebes.

TITANS. The sons of Uranus (heaven) and Gea (earth), who were defeated by Jupiter and cast into Tartarus.

TRALLES. A town in western Asia Minor.

TRIBUNE. One of several kinds of officers, civil and military; the Tribune of the People was sacrosanct.

TROJAN. In general, the descendants of Troy in Rome, whose ancestors had come with Aeneas and founded a colony in Italy, according to legend, in 1184 B.C.

TROY. An ancient city in northwest Asia Minor, whose king was Priam. After the abduction of Helen, wife of Menelaus, by Priam's son, Paris, the city was besieged by the combined Greek leaders for ten years.

TULLIUS. Servius Tullius, the sixth king of Rome (578–534 B.C.). He was one of the "good kings," followed by the Tarquins, who were eventually driven from Rome (510 B.C.), after which a republic was formed.

TULLUS. Tullus Hostilius, the third king of Rome (672–640 B.C.), who sacked and destroyed Alba Longa.

TURKISH. Juvenal says "Thracian."

TURNUS. King of the Rutulians, an ancient people in Latium; he was killed by Aeneas. In I Juvenal calls him "the fierce Rutulian." For Turnus and the Fury in VII see *Aeneid,* VII, 445 ff.; for the stone he threw in XV, see *Aeneid*, XII, 896–902.

TYNDARUS. Father of Clytemnestra, whose mother was Leda.

TYRE (Tyrian). A city on the coast of Phoenicia that produced fine and expensive purple fabrics dyed by a fluid secreted by the murex. Dido, who founded Carthage, was born here, and so Hannibal, in XII, is called "Tyrian."

TYRRHENIAN SEA. That part of the Mediterranean bordering Italy between Corsica and Sardinia on the north and Sicily on the south.

UCALEGON. A Trojan mentioned in Vergil's description of the burning of Troy (*Aeneid*, II, 310–12).

ULYSSES. Son of Laertes, prince of Ithaca, and the hero of the *Odyssey*. For his banquet with Alcinous, in XV, see *Odyssey,* VIII, 62 ff.

VASCONES. A tribe in Spain (ancestors of the contemporary Basques), north of the Ebro. The event referred to is the siege of their capital, Calagurris, by Afranius in 72 B.C.

VATICAN. One of the hills in Rome, which seems to have had large deposits of clay.

VEGETARIAN. Juvenal calls them Pythagoreans, who did not eat any sort of flesh. See the end of XV.

VEIENTO. Unknown in III and VI unless he is the same as Fabricius Veiento in IV, who was an informer under Domitian.

VENAFRAN. From Venafrum, an old town in Campania famous for its olive oil.

VENTIDIUS. P. Ventidius Bassus, son of a slave woman, who rose to be consul, 43 B.C. In XI, unknown.

VENUS. Goddess of love. In II the reference is to her being trapped in a net, while making love with Mars, by her legendary husband, Vulcan.

VERGIL. P. Vergilius Maro (70–19 B.C.), author of the *Aeneid* and other works.

VERGINIA. The beautiful daughter of L. Verginius, who stabbed her in the forum (449 B.C.) to save her from the lust of the decemvir, Appius Claudius (Livy, II).

VERGINIUS. Verginius Rufus, legate of Upper Germany, who defeated Vindex in his revolt against Nero, A.D. 68, and refused to be named emperor after Galba's death.

VERRES. Gaius Verres, praetor in Sicily (73–70 B.C.), who was tried for plundering the province. See Cicero's Verrine orations.

VESTA. Daughter of Saturn and Ops, goddess of the hearth and family life. Her temple in Alba was smaller than the great temple in Rome.

VESTINIAN. Relating to the Vestini, an ancient people of central Italy.

VINDEX. C. Julius Vindex, propraetor of the province of Lugdunensis in Gaul, who revolted against Nero, A.D. 68, and was defeated by Verginius Rufus.

VOLESUS. Meant to indicate in general the descendants of ancient nobility.

VOLSCIAN. Of a people in Latium on the banks of the Liris River. Arpinum was one of their towns.

VOLSINII. A town in Etruria.

VULCAN. God of fire, husband of Venus, son of Jupiter and Juno. He forged weapons, thunderbolts, etc., for the gods. His cave was in the (Aeolian) Lipari islands.

XERXES. King of Persia (c. 519–465 B.C.), son of Darius I and Atossa.

ZENO. Greek philosopher of Cyprus, founder of the Stoic school (c. 336–c. 264 B.C.).